SpringerBriefs in Law

SpringerBriefs present concise summaries of cutting-edge research and practical applications across a wide spectrum of fields. Featuring compact volumes of 50 to 125 pages, the series covers a range of content from professional to academic. Typical topics might include:

- A timely report of state-of-the art analytical techniques
- A bridge between new research results, as published in journal articles, and a contextual literature review
- A snapshot of a hot or emerging topic
- A presentation of core concepts that students must understand in order to make independent contributions

SpringerBriefs in Law showcase emerging theory, empirical research, and practical application in Law from a global author community. SpringerBriefs are characterized by fast, global electronic dissemination, standard publishing contracts, standardized manuscript preparation and formatting guidelines, and expedited production schedules.

Marina-Elissavet Konstantinidi

Closing the Gap: Enhancing the Implementation of Sustainable Development through International Investment Law

Springer

Marina-Elissavet Konstantinidi
LL.M., Attorney at Law
Piraeus Bar Association of Greece
Piraeus, Greece

ISSN 2192-855X ISSN 2192-8568 (electronic)
SpringerBriefs in Law
ISBN 978-3-031-73872-2 ISBN 978-3-031-73873-9 (eBook)
https://doi.org/10.1007/978-3-031-73873-9

This Springer imprint is published by the registered company Springer Nature Switzerland AG
The registered company address is: Gewerbestrasse 11, 6330 Cham, Switzerland

To Alexandra, Effie & Katerina
and to Anouk –
whose legacy keeps inspiring
May you rest in power.

Foreword

There is already a huge literature on the issue on International Investment Agreements, but until recently very little of this was directed to their impact on sustainable development in general or the UN Sustainable Development Goals in particular. So, it is a pleasure to recommend this short work to a wider audience.

International investment flows are vital to global development processes; naturally, investors need to feel that their investments are not subject to arbitrary changes in national law and policies. However, the world is changing; most notably, the "climate crisis" is looming larger and the world community needs, in extremely short order, to undergo a major realignment in its use of fossil fuels. An inevitable result will be investment disputes.

As Marina Konstantinidis points out, IIAs and the established arbitration processes that regulate them need to be able to respond more nimbly than at present to these major changes in public expectations. Important realignments of the global system are necessary to address, for example, the meaningful reduction of anthropogenic greenhouse emissions to the atmosphere. She provides us with a few important pointers to some key issues that need attention in such a realignment. She highlights the fact that there are already changes in State attitudes to Bilateral Investment treaties, but also flags the need for a change in practice in the interpretation of these agreements by arbitrators—itself linked to the need for a wider spread of expertise amongst the cohorts of professional arbitrators.

Washington, DC, USA
October 2024

David Freestone

Acknowledgments

The background work for the preparation of this book was carried out as part of a bigger project at the Centre de Droit International of the Free University of Brussels, which graciously hosted me as visiting researcher, while completing my Master's in Democritus University of Thrace.

My sincerest gratitude is owed to Prof. Nicolas Angelet for his guidance and for sparking my passion for legal research. I would also like to express my warmest thanks to Prof. David Freestone for his support and for graciously contributing the foreword to this book. My thanks extend to Prof. Aroni Chariklia and Prof. Konstantinos Antonopoulos, for their support throughout my Master's program. I am also profoundly thankful to Mrs. Charalambidou Natalia for her encouragement and enormously helpful feedback on earlier versions of this manuscript. I am grateful to the team of Springer for their constructive comments and support in publishing this book.

Lastly, my deepest gratitude goes to my family and close friends, for their unconditional love, trust, and support. Without them, I would not be who and where I am today.

All mistakes and omissions are the sole responsibility of the author.

Brussels, Belgium

Marina-Elissavet Konstantinidi

Contents

List of Abbreviations

BIT	Bilateral Investment Treaty
CETA	Comprehensive Economic and Trade Agreement
CSR	Corporate Social Responsibility
ECT	Energy Charter Treaty
EU	European Union
FDI	Foreign Direct Investment
FTA	Free Trade Agreement
GHG	Greenhouse Gas
ICJ	International Court of Justice
ICSID	International Centre for Settlement of Investment Disputes
IIA	International Investment Agreement
ILC	International Law Commission
ISDS	Investor State Dispute Settlement
NAFTA	North American Free Trade Agreement
NGO	Non-Governmental Organization
OECD	Organization for Economic Co-operation and Development
SOE	State-Owned Enterprise
UN	United Nations
UNCTAD	United Nations Conference on Trade and Development
VCLT	Vienna Convention on the Law of Treaties
WTO	World Trade Organization

Chapter 1
Introduction. Health and Environmental Protection in the Anthropocene

'We do not inherit the Earth from our ancestors; we borrow it from our children.'—*Native American Proverb*

Abstract The dawn of the Anthropocene unravelled major global challenges related to global health, ecological integrity and sustainability more broadly. Such challenges importantly call into question the role of International Investment Law as a means to protect foreign direct investments while reconciliating economic development and environmental protection. This introductory Chapter sets the stage for the book by examining relevant case studies that underscore points of conflict between public health and environmental emergencies and its relevance from an Investment Law perspective. Furthermore, it briefly analyses the concept of sustainable development from a conceptual framework to actionable goals, and explores the pivotal role that sustainable development plays within the context of international investment law. Finally, the Chapter outlines the methodological approach adopted in this book, providing insights into the analytical framework used to explore the intricate interplay between health, environmental conservation, and international investment law. Through these discussions, the Chapter aims to provide a comprehensive framework for bridging the gap between sustainable development and international investment law in the Anthropocene era.

1.1 Setting the Scene

December 3, 1984, India: about 45 tons of the dangerous gas methyl isocyanate (MIC) escape from an insecticide plant in Bhopal. The gas drifts over the densely populated neighborhoods around the plant, killing thousands of people immediately, and creating panic, as tens of thousands of others attempt to flee Bhopal. The final death toll is estimated to be between 15.000 and 20.000, while some half a million survivors suffer respiratory problems, eye irritation or blindness, and other maladies

M.-E. Konstantinidi, *Closing the Gap: Enhancing the Implementation of Sustainable Development through International Investment Law*, SpringerBriefs in Law,
https://doi.org/10.1007/978-3-031-73873-9_1

resulting from exposure to the toxic gas. Bhopal disaster, also referred to as the Bhopal Gas Tragedy, has been one of the worst industrial accidents in the world's history. Investigations later established that substandard operating and safety procedures at the understaffed plant had led to the catastrophe. The plant was owned by the Indian subsidiary of a foreign investor, the American firm Union Carbide Corporation.[1]

October 8, 1997, United States of America: The MTBE Public Health and Environment Protection Act of 1997 is signed into law in California, setting forth research topics involving the impact of methyl tertiary-butyl ether ("MTBE"), a compound used as a gasoline additive, on public health and the environment. The results of this research show that even low levels of MTBE can make water supplies undrinkable. Acute effects include headaches, nausea, dizziness, and disorientation, while laboratory animal experiments suggest it can cause maternal and fetal defects.[2] Further investigation demonstrated that MTBE leaked from underground tanker and pipelines, making its way into drinking water sources, and contaminating groundwater supplies of hundreds of communities across the state. Consequently, a ban on MTBE use is decided in the state of California to protect human health and the environment, affecting several corporations associated with MTBE's use. Amongst them is Methanex, a Canadian-owned company and a leading maker of methanol for the American market. Because of the Californian legislation, Methanex suffers a large loss of profit and follows the path of arbitration, seeking compensation.[3]

November 11, 2011, Australia: the Tobacco Plain Packaging Act (TPP Act)[4] is enacted by the Parliament of Australia, in accordance with the obligations that Australia had as a party to the World Health Organization's Framework Convention on Tobacco Control (FCTC),[5] aiming to reduce smoking. The TPP Act requires the removal of logos, brand imagery, colors, patterns, and promotional text on tobacco products and tobacco product packaging. Health cautions in pictures of diseases due to smoking should be displayed in 75% of the front and 90% of the back of tobacco packaging. All tobacco products sold in Australia have been required to comply with the legislation. Philip Morris Asia Limited (PM Asia), which is operating in Australia through a subsidiary, initiates an arbitration proceeding under the UNCITRAL Arbitration Rules at the Permanent Court of Arbitration in The Hague, on grounds that the plain packaging legislation had restricted the use of trademarks by Philip Morris Limited on its tobacco packaging, thus, constituting an

---

[1] Britannica (2020) Bhopal disaster industrial accident, Bhopal, India [1984]; Pant (2009).

[2] Concerns About MTBE, U.S. Envtl. Prot. Agency. Available at: http://www.epa.gov/mtbe/water.htm#concerns.

[3] *Methanex Corporation. v. United States of America*, UNCITRAL (1999).

[4] The Plain Packaging Act 2011 No. 148, 2011, An Act to Discourage the Use of Tobacco Products, and for related Purposes [Hereinafter Tobacco Plain Packaging Act 2011]. Available at: https://www.legislation.gov.au/Details/C2011A00148.

[5] WHO Framework Convention on Tobacco Control (FCTC) (May 21, 2003). WHA Res. 56.1, World Health Assembly 56th Ass., 4th plen. mtg, Agenda Item 13, Annex, WHO Doc. A56.VR/4, entered into force on 27 February 2005.

indirect expropriation.[6] The evolution of this case is part of the contemporary legal history.

A similar challenge modern societies have to face is global warming, which, according to a 2017 study, is by 100% connected to human activity.[7] Following the goals set by the Paris Agreement, States are taking mitigation measures to delay the catastrophic effects of climate change. However, such measures usually affect the activity of foreign investors, notably oil and coal companies, who have brought or threaten to bring investment arbitration claims against States on the grounds of breaching the applicable IIAs. Examples of such claims are provided by the cases of *WMH v. Canada,*[8] *Uniper v. Netherlands*[9] *and RWE v. Netherlands.*[10] Irrespective of the outcome of the arbitration proceedings, the risk of being ordered to pay very substantial damages may have a 'chilling effect' on States, meaning that they may hesitate to implement the energy transition measures needed to fight climate change and its consequences.[11]

The above-mentioned cases, although connected to different factual backgrounds, highlight a common problem: anthropogenic activity endangering the public goods of health and the environment. More specifically, the investment activity of transnational corporations in foreign territories raises the question of whether and to what extent this activity can be in line with the principles of sustainable development. The specific above-mentioned cases led or could have led to International Investment Arbitration for breach of the respective International Investment Agreements. This offers a glimpse of the existing challenges for the achievement of the Sustainable Development Goals, some of which occur when environmental and public health have to coexist with international investment treaties and the protections they offer to transnational investments.

[6] *Philip Morris Asia Limited v. The Commonwealth of Australia* (PCA Case No. 2012-12).

[7] Hausfather (2017).

[8] *Westmoreland Mining Holdings LLC v. Government of Canada*, ICSID Case No. UNCT/20/3.

[9] *Uniper SE, Uniper Benelux Holding B.V.* and *Uniper Benelux N.V. v. Kingdom of the Netherlands*, ICSID Case No. ARB/21/22; Connolly (2022).

[10] *AG and RWE Eemshaven Holding II BV v. Kingdom of the Netherlands*, ICSID Case No. ARB/21/4; Putter (2021).

[11] Brown and Miles (2011), pp. 134–135, 139–140; Baltag and Dautaj (2020), pp. 46–48; UNCTAD/ITE/IIA/2007/3, Investor-State Dispute Settlement and impact on investment rulemaking, United Nations, New York and Geneva (2007).

1.2 The Evolution of Sustainable Development: From Concept to Action

Sustainable development is a concept that has gathered increasing attention and significance in the global discourse over the last few decades. At its core, sustainable development embodies the idea of meeting the needs of the present without compromising the ability of future generations to meet their own needs.[12] Rooted in principles of economic prosperity, social equity, and environmental integrity, sustainable development reflects an evolving understanding of humanity's relationship with the planet.[13]

Historical precedents and movements advocating for environmental conservation and social justice have contributed to the development of modern sustainable development principles. From the conservation efforts of early environmentalists to indigenous approaches to stewardship, a rich tapestry of ideas and practices that laid the groundwork for modern sustainable development principles exists.[14] Despite its rapid evolution, it was not until the twentieth century that sustainable development emerged as a cohesive concept, with landmark events such as the 1972 Stockholm Conference on the Human Environment[15] and the 1992 Earth Summit in Rio de Janeiro,[16] which solidified sustainable development's place on the global agenda.[17]

Over time, the understanding of sustainable development has evolved, reflecting changing societal values and priorities. Initially focused primarily on environmental conservation, sustainable development has since expanded to encompass a broader array of concerns, including poverty alleviation, social equity, and cultural diversity.[18] This shift reflects a growing recognition of the interconnectedness of economic, social, and environmental systems, necessitating integrated approaches to sustainable development. International efforts, such as the adoption of the United Nations Sustainable Development Goals (SDGs) and the implementation of corporate social responsibility (CSR) initiatives, have sought to mainstream sustainability considerations into decision-making processes across various sectors.[19]

---

[12] Brutland Commission (1987) Report of the World Commission on Environment and Development: Our Common Future, p. 41.

[13] Griggs (2013).

[14] Cordonier Segger and Khalfan (2004).

[15] Stockholm Declaration on the Human Environment (1972). In: Report of the United Nations Conference on the Human Environment. UN Doc. A/CONF. 48/14.

[16] United Nations Conference on Environment and Development (1993). Rio de Janeiro, Brazil. Agenda 21: programme of action for sustainable development.

[17] Brisman (2011).

[18] Economic Commission for Latin America and the Caribbean (ECLAC) (2020) The 2030 Agenda for Sustainable Development in the new global and regional context: scenarios and projections in the current crisis. LC/PUB.2020/5, Santiago.

[19] United Nations (2018) The 2030 Agenda and the Sustainable Development Goals: An opportunity for Latin America and the Caribbean. LC/G. 2681-P/Rev. 3, Santiago; Carroll (2008); Besley and Ghatak (2007).

Despite progress in mainstreaming sustainable development, numerous challenges and critiques remain. Conflicts between economic growth and environmental conservation, disparities in access to resources, the persistence of unsustainable consumption and production patterns pose obstacles to the pursuit of sustainable development. Debates over the feasibility, measurability, and relevance of sustainable development continue to shape public discourses and policy-making, underlining the need for ongoing reflection and dialogue.

1.3 The Role of Sustainable Development in International Investment Law

As described above, sustainable development refers to the 'State's efforts to achieve progress (development), in a way that can be conserved over the long term (sustainable)'.[20] At the core of the concept of sustainable development is the integration principle, according to which, environmental concerns are integrated into economic development, while economic and social concerns are included reciprocally into environmental policies and obligations.[21]

As an expression of recognition of the importance of the principles of sustainable development by the international community, the objectives of sustainable development can be found more and more often enshrined in global economic agendas and multilateral and regional treaties.[22] This tendency is accompanied by intense debates. From a socio-environmental perspective, economic development stimulated through foreign direct investment shouldn't come at the expense of the States' right to regulate in the public interest. On the other hand, from an economic point of view, as outlined in Agenda 22 of the United Nations Conference on the Environment Development, '*investment is critical to the ability of developing countries to achieve needed economic growth to improve the welfare of their populations and to meet their basic needs in a sustainable manner, [...]. Sustainable development requires increased investment, for which domestic and external financial resources are needed*'[23]

Given the interconnected nature of economic, social and environmental aspects, achieving a balance of interests is crucial. In this context, the strong enforcement mechanisms provided by international investment law, if applied accordingly, have the potential to contribute to the protection of sustainable development.

---

[20] Segger and Newcombe (2010).

[21] Sands (2003), Montini (2023); InforMEA definition of the Integration principle. Available at: https://www.informea.org/en/terms/integration-principle.

[22] Lauterpacht (2010).

[23] UN (1992) United Nations Conference on Environment and Development (UNCED). Rio de Janeiro, Brazil, 3–14 June 1992.

The present book aims to contribute to this ongoing debate by outlining the key trends concerning the role of sustainable development in international investment law, raising, thereby, academic awareness on the issue. It explores if and how the tools offered by international investment law can be utilized to advance the United Nations Sustainable Development Goals.[24] In order to narrow down the scope of the research, the study specifically investigates how the notion of sustainable development affects the arguments concerning the existence of a protected investment, and the existence of an investment treaty violation. This analysis aims to shed light on how international investment law can support the goals of sustainable development, contributing to informed discussions and policy-making for a more equitable future.

1.4 Methodology

The methodology adopted in this book is anchored in legal analysis and scholarship, aiming to rigorously evaluate the intersection of international investment law and the sustainable development goals (SDGs). This approach incorporates systematic, analytical, and doctrinal methods to provide a comprehensive assessment of investment treaty practice within the context of investor-State dispute settlement (ISDS). Primary sources, including international treaties, statutes, court decisions, and regulations, are carefully examined to present the legal framework governing international investments. In parallel, secondary sources such as academic books, journal articles, and expert commentaries are consulted to provide additional depth and context to the analysis.

The book's analysis delves into the clauses of international investment agreements (IIAs) with particular relevance to the principles of sustainable development. Through meticulous examination of actual treaty language and pertinent precedents from arbitral case law, the book aims to offer an in-depth overview of the diverse approaches adopted by arbitral tribunals towards issues of sustainable development. Furthermore, by grounding the interpretation of IIAs in the Vienna Convention on the Law of Treaties (VCLT)[25] and the general principles of international law,[26] it is attempted to provide with potential pathways for employing the mechanism of investment arbitration in the efforts to protect human health and the environment.

Overall, the methodology adopted in this book is characterized by its comprehensive nature, aiming to provide nuanced insights into the interface between international investment law and sustainable development.

[24] Cotula (2014).

[25] Vienna Convention on the Law of the Treaties (1969).

[26] Third report of the Special Rapporteur, Mr. Marcelo Vázquez-Bermúdez (73rd session of the ILC (2022)). A/CN.4/753.

References

Baltag C, Dautaj Y (2020) Investors, states, and arbitrators in the crosshairs of international investment law and environmental protection. Brill Res Perspect Int Invest Law Arbitr 3(1): 1–77. https://doi.org/10.1163/24055778-12340008

Besley T, Ghatak M (2007) Retailing public goods: the economics of corporate social responsibility. J Public Econ 91(9):1645–1663

Brisman A (2011) Stockholm Conference, 1972. In: Chatterjee DK (ed) Encyclopedia of global justice. Springer, Dordrecht. https://doi.org/10.1007/978-1-4020-9160-5_655

Britannica T, Editors of Encyclopaedia (2020) Bhopal disaster industrial accident, Bhopal, India [1984]. Britannica. Available at: https://www.britannica.com/event/Bhopal-disaster

Brown C, Miles K (eds) (2011) Evolution in investment treaty law and arbitration. Cambridge University Press. https://doi.org/10.1017/CBO9781139043809

Carroll A (2008) A history of corporate social responsibility: concepts and practices. In: Crane A et al (eds) The Oxford handbook of corporate social responsibility. Oxford University Press, pp 19–46

Connolly K (2022) Olaf Scholz announces bailout for Germany's largest Russian gas importer. The Guardian. Available at: https://www.theguardian.com/world/2022/jul/22/olaf-scholz-announces-bailout-for-germanys-largest-russian-gas-importer-uniper

Cordonier Segger MC, Khalfan A (2004) Origins of the sustainable development concept. In: Sustainable development law: principles, practices, and prospects. OUP. https://doi.org/10.1093/acprof:oso/9780199276707.003.0002

Cotula L (2014) Investment treaties and sustainable development: investor-state arbitration. IIED. Available at: https://pubs.iied.org/pdfs/17241IIED.pdf

Griggs D et al (2013) Sustainable development goals for people and planet. Nature 495:305–307. https://doi.org/10.1038/495305a

Hausfather Z (2017) Analysis: why scientists think 100% of global warming is due to humans. CarbonBrief. Available at: https://www.carbonbrief.org/analysis-why-scientists-think-100-of-global-warming-is-due-to-humans/

Lauterpacht E (2010) Foreword. In: Segger M, Gehring M, Newcombe A (eds) Sustainable development in world investment law. Kluwer Law International, Alphen aan de Rijn

Montini M (2023) The principle of integration. In: Faure M (ed) Elgar encyclopedia of environmental law. Chap VI.10. https://doi.org/10.4337/9781785365669.VI.10

Pant M (2009) Foreign investment & Bhopal tragedy. The Economic Times, Opinion. https://economictimes.indiatimes.com/opinion/et-commentary/foreign-investment-bhopal-tragedy/articleshow/5324524.cms?from=mdr

Putter S (2021) The Netherlands Coal Phase-Out and the Resulting (RWE and Uniper) ICSID Arbitrations. Kluwer Arbitration Blog. Available at: https://arbitrationblog.kluwerarbitration.com/2021/08/24/the-netherlands-coal-phase-out-and-the-resulting-rwe-and-uniper-icsid-arbitrations/

Sands P (2003) Principles of international environmental law, vol 2. Cambridge University Press

Segger M, Newcombe A (2010) An integrated agenda for sustainable development in international investment law. In: Segger M, Gehring M, Newcombe A (eds) Sustainable development in world investment law. Kluwer Law International, Alphen aan de Rijn

Chapter 2
Sustainable Development Goals and the Existence of a Protected Investment

> The environment and the economy are really both two sides of the same coin. If we cannot sustain the environment, we cannot sustain ourselves.—*Wangari Maathai*

Abstract This Chapter explores the evolving landscape of Investment Treaty clauses related to sustainable development, and offers an overview of the gradual emergence of various types of environment-related provisions across the international investment legal framework. First, it examines specific provisions of International Investment Agreements (IIAs) referring explicitly to sustainable development. As shown herein, such reference is a relatively recent development, gaining prominence since the 1990s, and becoming an arguably emerging objective nowadays. While not the primary tool for promoting sustainability, such treaty provisions, play a critical role in defining which foreign investments can be granted protection. The Chapter further dissects the long-standing definition of 'protected investment' under IIAs as developed in *Salini v. Morocco* case. More specifically, the analysis focuses on the requirement for an investment to be in accordance with host State law and to contribute to its economic development. By reference to relevant case law, this Chapter aims to outline potential defensive strategies for States facing investment treaty claims and, ultimately, to support the implementation of climate policies and the enforcement of sustainable development objectives.

2.1 International Investment Agreements Making Reference to Sustainable Development

The international community acknowledges the importance of the principles inspired by sustainable development by increasingly integrating the objectives of sustainable development in global economic agendas and multilateral and regional

M.-E. Konstantinidi, *Closing the Gap: Enhancing the Implementation of Sustainable Development through International Investment Law*, SpringerBriefs in Law,
https://doi.org/10.1007/978-3-031-73873-9_2

treaties.[1] Although it was not traditionally a common phenomenon for BITs to carry sustainable development-related provisions, the scenario has transformed over the past years.[2] Depending on their context, these provisions create obligations for the investors that may determine whether an investment shall be covered by an IIA, and, thereby, enjoy the relevant protections.

IIAs including an environmental protection clause may have distinct ways of framing such obligations. Certain BITs use the form of a general exception clause modelled in the form of Article XX (General Exceptions) of the General Agreement on Tariffs and Trade (GATT).[3] Other BITs contain specific clauses addressing the objectives of states. For example, the Canada-Republic of Moldova BIT under its Article 15 lists health, safety and environmental measures as being important for both States, stating that no measure must be taken in derogation of these objectives.[4] Other BITs, such as the Australia-Uruguay Treaty, list these objectives from the preamble itself.[5]

Furthermore, many BITs exclude environmental provisions from being subject to arbitration, although this seems to be changing. For example, the Iran-Slovakia BIT permits parties to use the investor-state dispute settlement (ISDS) mechanism when a state breaches its non-regression obligations.[6] This evolution may facilitate claims by investors in cases where states weaken their environmental protection laws, including where states roll back regulations aimed at reducing greenhouse gas emissions. In a different example, the environmental-related obligations imposed by the 2016 Morocco-Nigeria BIT on investors include the requirement to apply the 'precautionary principle' when assessing the environmental impact of an investment. Under the precautionary principle, when there is a risk of serious environmental damage, lack of scientific certainty does not justify an investor postponing preventative measures.[7]

Another example can be found in the Energy Charter Treaty, which, under its Article 19 states that:

> In pursuit of sustainable development and taking into account its obligations under those international agreements concerning the environment.

---

[1] Levashova (2011), pp. 222–229; Collins and Sharpe (2022).

[2] Organisation for Economic Cooperation and Development (2011) Environmental Concerns in International Investment Agreement. OECD Working Papers on International Investment 2011/01. Available at: https://www.oecd.org/investment/internationalinvestmentagreements/WP-2011_1.pdf.

[3] Such an example is offered by Article 10 of Canada-Peru BIT (2007).

[4] Agreement between the Government of Canada and the Government of the Republic of Moldova for the Promotion and Protection of Investments, Article 15. Health, Safety and Environmental Measures.

[5] Agreement between Australia and the Oriental Republic of Uruguay on the Promotion and Protection of Investments.

[6] Mitchell and Munro (2018), p. 625.

[7] UNCTAD. Mapping of IIA clauses. Investment Policy Hub. Available at: https://investmentpolicy.unctad.org/pages/1031/mapping-of-iia-clauses.

The provision moves further to include the international environmental principle 'the polluter should pay':

> In its policies and actions each Contracting Party shall strive to take precautionary measures to prevent or minimise environmental degradation. The Contracting Parties agree that the polluter in the Areas of Contracting Parties, should, in principle, bear the cost of pollution, including transboundary pollution, with due regard to the public interest.[8]

However, despite the generally observed shift towards inclusion of environmental obligations, as clauses are very generic, the obligations upon investors remain unclear. For instance, the 2012 US Model BIT includes in its preamble the following provision: '*Desiring to achieve these objectives in a manner consistent with the protection of health, safety, and the environment*' providing fertile ground for broad interpretation as to the precise obligation expectations.[9]

To better analyse the impact of these references to sustainable development in practice, we will examine how arbitral tribunals have used such references in their argumentation. More specifically, the following section focuses on the definition of investment as a prerequisite for the enjoyment of the protections provided under the relevant IIA and the establishment of jurisdiction of the competent tribunals.

2.1.1 *Definition of a 'Protected Investment' According to the ICSID Convention*

A crucial element for the establishment of an investment tribunal's jurisdiction is for the investment to fall under the scope of the definition provided by the relevant IIA. If no investment falls under the scope of the definition provided, no protection can be granted.[10]

Under the ICSID Convention, jurisdiction is governed by Article 25(1), which reads as follows:

> The jurisdiction of the Centre shall extend to any legal dispute arising directly out of an investment between a Contracting State (or any constituent subdivision or agency of a Contracting State designated to the Centre by that State) and a national of another Contracting State, which the parties to the dispute consent in writing to submit to the Centre. When the parties have given their consent, no party may withdraw its consent unilaterally.[11]

[8] Energy Charter Treaty (1994) Signed on 17 December. Available at: https://www.energycharter.org/fileadmin/DocumentsMedia/Legal/ECTC-en.pdf.

[9] 2012 U.S. Model Bilateral Investment Treaty. Treaty between the United States of America and the Government of [Country] concerning the encouragement and reciprocal protection of investment.

[10] Levashova (2011) id., pp. 1–2.

[11] International Centre for Settlement of Investment Disputes (2003) Article 25. ICSID Convention. Regulations and Rules. Washington, D.C.

With the prerequisite that ICSID Convention is applicable at relevant times, for a tribunal to have jurisdiction under Article 25(1) of the ICSID Convention, four conditions shall, therefore, be satisfied: (i) the arbitration must be between a Contracting State and a national of another Contracting State, (ii) there must be a legal dispute arising directly out of (iii) an investment, and (iv) the Contracting State and the investor must have consented in writing to ICSID arbitration. The tribunal established on the basis of an investment treaty has the duty to verify its jurisdiction under that treaty, even if the parties have not objected to it.

The present chapter elaborates on the prerequisite of existence of an investment, and how it may be connected to the principles of sustainable development. It focuses on the requirement for an investment to be '*in accordance with the host State law*' and the element of '*contribution to the economic development of the host State*' by reference to IIAs and arbitral case-law.

2.2 Contribution to the Economic Development of the Host State

In the 1990s, arbitrators had defined investment according to the following criteria: i) existence of a financial contribution; ii) term of a project; iii) purpose of the project; iv) involvement of an investor into the project management and v) risk inherent in the project.[12] However, the scope of responsibilities for the investment remained quite limited.

Different analytical tools have been used in order to determine which investments should be protected under the ICSID/BIT mechanism. Among these tools a more obejctive one, was adopted in the case *Salini v Morocco.*[13] According to the so-called 'Salini test', which elaborates certain criteria already mentioned in *Fedax v. Venezuela*, an investment should have the following features: i) asset contribution; ii) risk inherent in the project; iii) long duration and iv) contribution to economy of the host state.[14]

By introducing the fourth element, the tribunal *de facto* enlarged the scope of investors' responsibilities towards the host State. It is worth mentioning that some tribunals see contribution to economy as a consequence of investment, but not an essential feature thereof. The Salini test has been widely cited for the reason that it provides a predictable, simple, and uniform rule. This gives the possibility to a tribunal to dismiss and investor's claim on jurisdictional grounds if the foreign

[12] Schefer (2013), pp. 59–60.

[13] *Salini Costruttori S.P.A. and Italstrade S.P.A. v Kingdom of Morocco*. ICSID Case No. ARB/00/4.

[14] Grabowski (2014), pp. 302–304.

investment, *inter alia,* does not significantly contribute to development of the host State's economy.[15]

There has been wide controversy among tribunals regarding the definition of a protected investment, especially with respect to the element of *'contribution to the economic development of the host State'*. Certain cases argue that contribution to the economic development of the host State is not a condition for the existence of a protected investment, while other cases bring attention to the difficulty of establishing an 'economic contribution to the host state' on a practical level.[16]

Many tribunals have supported the position expressed in Salini case, including the element of economic development in their assessment. However, it should be noted that the Salini test is not absolute in investment arbitration. Some tribunals have indeed followed this test, while others only accepted the first three criteria.[17] Furthermore, as Professor Stern observes,[18] the Salini test is sometimes denounced as too rigid. In any case, though, the additional comment the tribunal in *Salini* made, shouldn't be disregarded:

> In reality, these various elements may be interdependent ... [a]s a result, these various criteria should be assessed globally.[19]

A similar approach was followed by the tribunal in *Jan de Nul v. Egypt*:

> The ICSID Convention contains no definition of the term "investment". The Tribunal concurs with ICSID precedents which, subject to minor variations, have relied on the so-called "Salini test". Such test identifies the following elements as indicative of an "investment" for purposes of the ICSID Convention: (i) a contribution, (ii) a certain duration over which the project is implemented, (iii) a sharing of operational risks, and (iv) a contribution to the host State's development, being understood that these elements may be closely interrelated, should be examined in their totality and will normally depend on the circumstances of each case.[20]

Regardless of the approach followed by tribunals, the contribution to the host State's economic development remains an important element in the tribunals' assessment. The concept of economic development is comprised of goals like Gross National Product growth, quality of life, promotion of welfare and development of communities within the host State and other subjective goals of States, including the SDGs.[21] A question relevant for the purposes of the present study is whether and

[15] Schefer (2013), p. 89

[16] Grabowski (2014) id. p. 298.

[17] Stern (2011), p. 536.

[18] Ibid.

[19] *Salini Costruttori S.P.A. and Italstrade S.P.A. v Kingdom of Morocco*. ICSID Case No. ARB/00/4, para. 52.

[20] *Jan de Nul N.V. and Dredging International N.V. v. Arab Republic of Egypt*. ICSID Case No. ARB/04/13, Decision on Jurisdiction, (June 16, 2006). para. 91.

[21] Dang and Pheng (2015); Mukherjee and Chakrabarti (2021), pp. 429–463.

to what extent economic development in this context should abide by the principles of sustainable development.

Increasing recognition that the overall goals of environmental conservation and economic development should and can be mutually reinforcing has prompted calls for recognizing in practice the concept of 'sustainable economic development'.[22] The importance of promoting inclusive and sustainable economic growth is already depicted in Goal 8 of the SDGs.[23] However, in the context of international investment law, such link has not expressly been reflected in any legislative text until now. It remains upon the interpretative discretion of investment tribunals to define the content of economic development and the investors' expected contribution to it.

Following this reasoning, the present section elaborates on how investment tribunals take into account the concept of economic development for the definition of a protected investment under the respective treaty.

2.2.1 Economic Development and the ICSID Convention

The position in favor of including economic development in the assessment concerning the definition of 'investment' can find support in the ICSID Convention, which is considered 'an instrument of international policy for the promotion of economic development'.[24] Indeed, the ICSID Convention addresses the question of the purpose of IIAs in its preamble:

> Considering the need for international cooperation for economic development, and the role of private international investment therein.[25]

Furthermore, the report from the Executive Directors underlines the need for mutual respect of the interests of both investors and States, while promoting the inflow of investments:

> 12. . .Adherence to the Convention by a country would provide additional inducement and stimulate a larger flow of private international investment into its territories, which is the primary purpose of the Convention.

[22] Barbier (1987), pp. 101–110; Balisacan et al. (2014). Available at: https://www.elsevier.com/books/sustainable-economic-development/balisacan/978-0-12-800347-3; Beirne and Fernandez (2022).

[23] UN Goal 8: Promote inclusive and sustainable economic growth, employment and decent work for all. Available at: https://unric.org/en/sdg-8/; UNESDA also refers to the concept of 'Sustainable Economic Development' as a priority area in its SIDS 2014 Partnerships Platform. Available at: https://sdgs.un.org/publications/sids-partnerships-briefs-sustainable-economic-development-17785.

[24] UNCTAD (2011) Scope and Definition. UNCTAD Series on Issues in International Investment Agreements II, UN NY & Geneva.

[25] International Centre for Settlement of Investment Disputes (2003) ICSID Convention. Regulations and Rules. Washington, D.C.

> 13...The provisions of the Convention maintain a careful balance between the interests of investors and those of host States.[26]

The element of economic development is also apparent in the relationship between ICSID and the World Bank, depicted in the preamble of the ICSID Convention: *'Desiring to establish such facilities under the auspices of the International Bank for Reconstruction and Development.'*[27] The International Bank for Reconstruction and Development (IBRD), which is one of the entities that comprise the World Bank, has, among others, as its purpose to facilitate and encourage international investment for: (a) productive purposes; (b) for the development of the productive resources of countries to increase productivity, standards of living and conditions of labour.[28] It can, thus, be argued, that since investments not devoted to the above purposes contradict with the objectives of the World Bank, they should not be covered by the protections of ICSID.[29] This means that investments made for the sole purpose of private profit, not developing the productive resources of the host State cannot actually be considered 'investments' under the respective IIAs.

Apart from sharing premises,[30] ICSID and the World Bank have a financial and operational linkage. Any excess in expenditure which the Centre cannot meet shall be borne by the Bank,[31] while the president of the Bank is also the chairman of the Administrative Council of ICSID, with the authority, among others, to appoint arbitrators in given circumstances.[32] In this context, the developmental benefits of investment inflows for host States cannot be disregarded. Therefore, ICSID, being inextricably linked to the World Bank, includes in its essence the element of economic development.

---

[26] Report of the Executive Directors of the International Bank for Reconstruction and Development on the Convention on the Settlement of Investment Disputes between States and Nationals of other States (1965) 4 I.L.M; Report of the Executive Directors on the Convention on the Settlement of Investment Disputes between States and Nationals of Other States (2012) The History of ICSID. Oxford Oxford Academic. Available at: https://doi.org/10.1093/acprof:oso/9780199660568.005.0005.

[27] Preamble, Convention on the Settlement of Investment Disputes between States and Nationals of Other States (ICSID Convention) (1965).

[28] International Bank for Reconstruction and Development (IBRD) Articles of Agreement (1989): Article I, The World Bank. Available at: https://www.worldbank.org/en/about/articles-of-agreement/ibrd-articles-of-agreement/article-I.

[29] Garcia-Bolivar (2011), p. 591.

[30] Convention on the Settlement of Investment Disputes between States and Nationals of Other States (1965) Article 2.

[31] Ibid., Article 17.

[32] Convention on the Settlement of Investment Disputes between States and Nationals of Other States (1965) Article 5.

2.2.2 International Investment Agreements Referring to Economic Development

As already mentioned, more and more IIAs explicitly refer to the concept of sustainable development. Similarly, and with greater historical continuity, economic development is pervasive in the text of IIAs. However, it is not clear if such contribution is a prerequisite for an investment to fall under the scope of the respective IIA. One should examine each case separately, taking into account the interpretative tools offered by VCLT.

For instance, the Energy Charter Treaty, a multilateral treaty which includes provisions on the promotion and protection of investments, states in its preamble that the purpose of the Charter's measures to liberalise the energy sector is to promote economic development likened to economic growth:

> Wishing to implement the basic concept of the European Energy Charter initiative which is to catalyse economic growth by means of measures to liberalize investment and trade in energy.[33]

Despite the highly opposed views regarding the interests served by the ECT,[34] and the recent practice of States,[35] its primary purpose of promoting and protecting investments has a direct connection to economic development. In the explanatory note reference is even made to sustainable development: *'Recognising the global challenge posed by the trilemma between energy security, economic development and environmental protection, and efforts by all countries to achieve sustainable development'*.[36] Furthermore, reference is made to the notion of sustainable development in the preamble of the ECT:

> *'Willing to do more to attain the objectives of energy security and efficient management and use of resources, and to utilise fully the potential for environmental improvement, in moving towards sustainable development'*.[37] At the same time, it is mentioned that it is within the ECT objectives to take action for cooperation in the energy field, entailing, amongst others, *'formulation of stable and transparent legal frameworks creating conditions for the development of energy resources in the context of sustainable development'*.[38]

On the other side of the globe, the North America Free Trade Agreement (NAFTA) serves as another example of an IIA whose obligations should be considered in a broader context. Even if NAFTA does not explicitly mention economic development

[33] The Energy Charter Treaty (1994). Available at: https://www.energycharter.org/process/energy-charter-treaty-1994/energy-charter-treaty/.

[34] IISD Statement (2022) Energy Charter Treaty Withdrawal Announcements Reflect Reform Outcome is Insufficient for Climate Ambition. Available at: https://www.iisd.org/articles/statement/energy-charter-treaty-withdrawal-announcements.

[35] Ballantyne (2022).

[36] The Energy Charter Treaty, op. cit., p. 11.

[37] Id., p. 12.

[38] Id., p. 13.

within its scope, a look at its objective and preambular statements indicates that the focus of NAFTA goes beyond investment promotion and includes wider social, human rights and environmental aspects.[39] As stated, States resolve to:

> CONTRIBUTE to the harmonious development and expansion of world trade and provide a catalyst to broader international cooperation; . . .
> ENSURE a predictable commercial framework for business planning and investment; . . .
> UNDERTAKE each of the preceding in a manner consistent with environmental protection and conservation;
> PRESERVE their flexibility to safeguard the public welfare;
> PROMOTE sustainable development;
> STRENGTHEN the development and enforcement of environmental laws and regulations; and
> PROTECT, enhance and enforce basic workers' rights

Similarly, the BIT between Cuba and the United Kingdom illustrates the intention of the parties to create favourable conditions for foreign investment while recognising that the agreement will '*contribute to the stimulation of business initiative and will increase prosperity in both States*'.[40] References to the intention of promoting economic growth are also contained in the BIT between Germany and Israel, which mentions the effect that investor protection will have on mutual prosperity.[41] Other BITs, such as the Spain-China[42] and Sweden-Venezuela[43] BITs include within their objectives the development of economic co-operation between their parties.

In an attempt to express the intention of States when entering such agreements, the US Model BIT recognises that '*agreement on the treatment to be accorded such investment will stimulate the flow of private capital and the economic development of the parties*' mentioning that State parties agree that '*a stable framework for investment will maximize effective utilization of economic resources and improve living standards*'.[44] Even though the unclear language of the text of the treaty may give rise to different interpretations, the specific reference to economic development in the preamble provides the context needed for identifying the purpose of the BIT. Bringing the concept of sustainable development to the table, IISD has developed

---

[39] Garcia-Bolivar (2011) id., p. 593.

[40] Agreement between the Government of the United Kingdom of Great Britain and Northern Ireland and the Government of the Republic of Cuba for the Promotion and Protection of Investments, signed on 30 January 1995 (entered into force 11 May 1995).

[41] Treaty between the Federal Republic of Germany and the State of Israel concerning the Encouragement and Reciprocal Protection of Investments, signed on 24 June 1976.

[42] Agreement between the People's Republic of China and the Kingdom of Spain on the Promotion and Reciprocal Protection of Investments (entered into force 1 July 2008).

[43] Agreement between the Government of the Kingdom of Sweden and the Government of the Republic of Venezuela on the Promotion and the Reciprocal Protection of Investments, signed on 25 November 1996 (entered into force on January 5, 1998).

[44] Treaty between the Government of the United States of America and the Government of [Country] Concerning the Encouragement and Reciprocal Protection of Investment [US BIT Model (2004)].

a positive negotiations agenda that '*establishes the aspirations of developing countries and the promotion of global sustainable development as a clear purpose for the international agreement*'[45]

However, the majority of IIAs limit their purpose to the promotion and protection of foreign investment making it almost compulsory for arbitral tribunals to engage in a deeper teleological interpretation to determine the definition of a protected investment. To better understand the existing controversies, it is important to examine the reasoning followed by arbitrators who have recognized the importance of promoting investments that contribute to economic, or even sustainable development of host States, which is what the following section intends to do.

2.2.3 *The Concept of Economic Development in the Jurisprudence of Arbitral Tribunals*

The relevance of economic development with the existence of a protected investment has been analysed by arbitral tribunals to a large extent with regards to the purpose of the ICSID Convention. The preambular statement of ICSID Convention occupies a central position in this analysis.[46] Since there is no specific definition of the term 'investment', certain criteria have been developed in jurisprudence to determine when an investment falls under the corresponding BIT.

In the identification of these criteria, the most representative case known to date is the *Salini Costruttori SpA and Italstrade SpA v. Moroco.*[47] As already mentioned above, the 'Salini test' indicated the following criteria: '*contributions, a certain duration of performance of the contract, and a participation in the risks of the transaction*'[48] noting that '*one may add the contribution to the economic development of the host State of the investment as an added condition*'.[49] In relation to contribution to the economic development the tribunal commented that '*in most countries, the construction of infrastructure falls under the tasks to be carried out by the State or by other public authorities.*' It added that '*the highway in question shall serve the public interest*' and that the companies in question '*were also able to provide the host State of the investment with know-how in relation to the work to be accomplished*'.[50]

[45] IISD Model International Agreement on Investment for Sustainable Development. Available at: https://www.iisd.org/publications/guide/iisd-model-international-agreement-investment-sustainable-development.

[46] UNCTAD, Scope and Definition (2011) id., p. 52.

[47] *Salini Costruttori SpA and Italstrade SpA v. Morocco*, ICSID Case No. ARB/00/4, Decision on Jurisdiction of 23 July 2001.

[48] Id., para. 52.

[49] Ibid.

[50] Id., para. 57.

A further criterion was identified by the tribunal in *Malaysian Historical Salvors Sdn Bhd v. Malaysia (MHS)*:[51] the enhancement of the GDP of the local economy. In this award, which was subsequently annulled by an ad hoc Annulment Committee, a significant contribution to the economic development of the host State was considered a requirement for the investment to enjoy the protection of the relevant BIT. As stated:

> The weight of the authorities cited above swings in favour of requiring a significant contribution to be made to the host State's economy. Were there not the requirement of significance, any contract which enhances the Gross Domestic Product of an economy by any amount, however small, would qualify as an 'investment.'[52]

It is worth mentioning the dissenting opinion of Judge Mohamed Shahabuddeen in the ad hoc Committee annulling the award.[53] He strongly criticized the decision, commenting that:

> An ICSID investment might indeed be made in favour of private entities but not for their own enrichment exclusively: only on the basis that, though made in favour of private entities, such an investment would – not might – promote the economic development of the host State.[54]

He further referred to the preamble of the ICSID Convention mentioning that it

> reflects an inference that the very purpose of an ICSID investment is to contribute to the economic development of the host State ... it is not merely that 'international investment plays a role in economic development' of the host State: international investment must play a role in the economic development of the host State if the investment is to rank as an ICSID investment and be entitled to the protection of the ICSID settlement procedures; that requirement is a condition of an ICSID investment.[55]

In an opposite direction, the tribunal in *Pey Casado v. Chile* goes against the reading of a 'contribution to economic development' as an essential component of an investment. As stated:

> According to the tribunal, this definition comprises only three elements. The requirement of a contribution to the economic development of the host State, which is difficult to measure, seems to be a central element in the disputes, and not of the competence of the tribunal. It is true that the Preamble to the ICSID Convention mentions the contribution to the economic development of the host State. However, this reference is presented as a consequence and not as a condition of the investment: by protecting investments, the Convention facilitates the development of the host State. This does not mean that the development of the host State is a

[51] *Malaysian Historical Salvors Sdn Bhd v. Malaysia*, ICSID Case No. ARB/05/10, Award on Jurisdiction (17 May 2007).

[52] Id., para 123.

[53] UNCTAD, Scope and Definition (2011) UNCTAD Series on Issues in International Investment Agreements II. UN NY & Geneva, p. 64.

[54] *Malaysian Historical Salvors Sdn Bhd v. Malaysia*, ICSID Case No. ARB/05/10, Decision on Annulment of 16 April 2009, Dissenting Opinion of Judge Mohamed Shahabuddeen, para 17.

[55] Id., paras 28–29.

> constitutive element of the notion of investment. This is why, as was noted by certain arbitral tribunals, this fourth condition is in reality encompassed by the first three.[56]

In the case *Romak v. Uzbekistan* the tribunal analysed the term 'investment' by reference to the interpretative tools provided by the VCLT. It noted that '*the Arbitral Tribunal needs to construe the term "investments" in its context and in light of the object and purpose of the BIT.* '[57] It drew attention to the BIT's preamble, and to the definition of the term "*returns*"... *the repeated references to "territory".. in relation with the investment.., and the description of the protection offered at Article 3(1), all of which denote an economic activity involving some permanence or duration in relation to the host State.* '[58] Even though the tribunal discarded the requirement of a contribution to the host State's economic development , it considered that the term 'investments' under the respective BIT '*has an inherent meaning, entailing a contribution that extends over a certain period of time and that involves some risk*'[59]

In *Amco v. Indonesia* it was concluded that:

> The Convention is aimed to protect, to the same extent and with the same vigour the investor and the host State, not forgetting that to protect investments is to protect the general interest of development and of developing countries.[60]

Later on, in *Ceskoslovenska obchodni banka, a.s. v. Slovak Republic (CSOB)* the tribunal stated that the investment should have a positive impact on the host State's development. It concluded that the preamble of the ICSID Convention '*permits an inference that an international transaction which contributes to cooperation designed to promote the economic development of a Contracting State may be deemed to be an investment as that term is understood in the Convention*'[61]

Following the above analysis, certain factors identified to be contributing to the economic development of the host State include the following: (a) the investment should be beneficial to the public interest, (b) there should be some transfer of know-how, (c) it should enhance the GDP of the local economy, (d) have a positive impact on the host State's development.

[56] *Victor Pey Casado and President Allende Foundation v. Republic of Chile*, ICSID Case No. ARB/98/2, para 232.

[57] *Romak SA (Switzerland) v. Republic of Uzbekistan*, PCA Case No. AA280, Award of 26 November 2009, para 197.

[58] Ibid.

[59] Id., para. 207.

[60] *Amco Asia Corporation v. Indonesia*, ICSID Case No. ARB/81/1, Decision on Jurisdiction of 25 September 1983.

[61] *Ceskoslovenska obchodni banka, a.s. v. Slovak Republic*, ICSID Case No. ARB/97/4, Decision on Jurisdiction of 24 May 1999, para. 64.

2.2.4 Conclusion

The discourse concerning the concept of economic development is accompanied by the interpretation of the nature and purpose of the ICSID Convention. Some tribunals argue that ICSID jurisdiction is solely based on the applicable BIT.[62] Others, as analysed above, have concluded that Article 25(1) introduces certain objective requirements, among which is the contribution to the economic development, which have to be present for a transaction to come within the meaning of "investment".

In the adjudication of ISDS cases, when interpreting the concept of economic development and attempting to define the term 'investment', States' intention should be taken into account. An interpretation in accordance with the object and the purpose of ICSID and is good faith should also recognise the importance of sustainable economic growth and support instruments in this respect.[63] This way, a step closer to the realization of SDGs can be achieved.

2.3 The Legality Requirement

Another element bringing controversy to the definition of 'investment' is the 'legality requirement'. The prerequisite for an investment to be 'in accordance with the host State law' can be found differently framed in many BITs. Investment tribunals consider such clauses in general as having the effect of excluding illegal investment from protection under the relevant BIT.[64] Such an approach, even though not unanimous in jurisprudence, can serve a mechanism available for host States to defend against investment treaty claims, and, consequently, influence the implementation of the principles of sustainable development.

2.3.1 International Investment Agreements Promoting 'Legal' Investments

Many investment protection treaties contain clauses on the conformity of the investment with host State law. The wording of these clauses can, however, differ significantly, both in terms of wording and in terms of the part of the IIA they are located. In most cases, they concern the definition of the term 'investment'.[65] The

[62] UNCTAD. Scope and Definition (2011) id., pp. 52–53.

[63] Garcia-Bolivar (2011) id., p. 589.

[64] Carlevaris (2008), pp. 35–49.

[65] Kriebaum (2010).

purpose of such provisions is to ensure the integrity of the ICSID regime,[66] and '*prevent the Bilateral Treaty from protecting investments that should not be protected, particularly because they would be illegal*', as was explained by the Tribunal in *Salini v. Morocco*.[67]

In general, European countries do not grant a right of admission but limit themselves to standards and guarantees for those investments which the host State has unilaterally decided to admit. A typical clause of this kind reads: '*Each Contracting Party shall in its territory promote as far as possible investments by investors of the other Contracting State and admit such investments in accordance with its legislation.*'[68]

Article I (2) of the Argentina-United States BIT contains the following:

> The term 'investment' shall mean every kind of asset, including property and rights of any kind acquired or affected in accordance with the laws of the receiving State, including, although not exclusively.[69]

Similarly, Article 1 (1) of the Sri Lanka model BIT mentions that

> The term 'investment' means every kind of property or asset invested by an investor of one Contracting Party in the territory of the other Contracting Party in accordance with the laws and regulations of the Contracting Party . . .

As can be observed in Fig. 2.1, the majority of BITs contain '*in accordance with host State law*' clauses, though anti-corruption clauses are on the rise in new-generation BITs.

At the same time, about two-thirds of all BITs signed between 1959 and 2016 include in their text the requirement that the investment must be made '*in accordance with host State law*' (see Fig. 2.2).[70]

It is interesting to note that many BITs require additionally that the investment must be *admitted* in accordance with host State law. A recent few BITs broaden the scope of this provision by adding the additional requirement for the investment tobe *made and operated* in accordance with host State laws.[71]

---

[66] Aceris Law LLC. (2018) The Salini Test in ICSID Arbitration. Available at: https://www.acerislaw.com/the-salini-test-in-icsid-arbitration.

[67] *Salini Costruttori S.P.A. and Italstrade S.P.A. v. Kingdom of Morocco*, ICSID Case No. ARB/00/4, Decision on Jurisdiction, 23 July 2001, 6 ICSID Reports 400, para 46.

[68] Germany Model Bilateral Investment Treaty (2005), Art. 2(1).

[69] Treaty between United States of America and the Argentine Republic concerning the Reciprocal Encouragement and protection Investment, Article I (2).

[70] Ibid.

[71] Id.

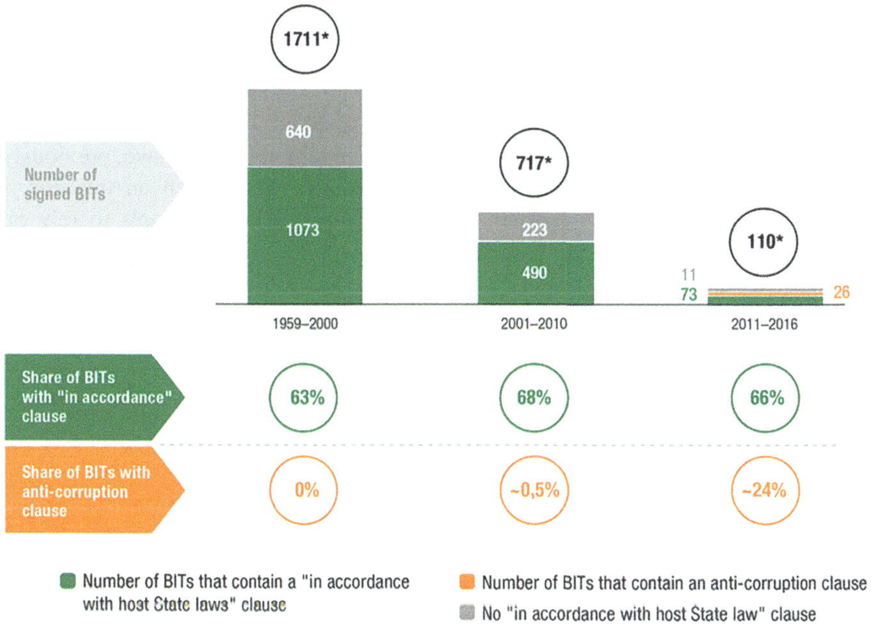

Fig. 2.1 BITs containing an "in accordance with host State law" and/or "anti-corruption" clause. Source: © UNCTAD, IIA Mapping Project. Based on 2'538 BITs signed between 1959 and 2016 (UNCTAD. Mapping of IIA Clauses. Investment Policy Hub. Available at: https://investmentpolicy.unctad.org/pages/1031/mapping-of-iia-clauses)

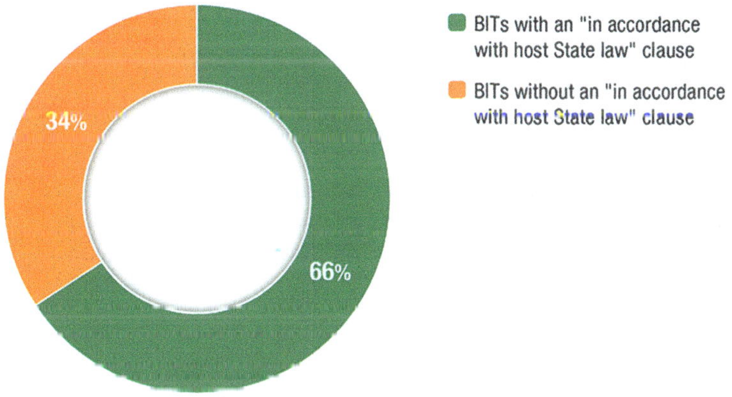

Fig. 2.2 BITs with and without an "in accordance with host State law" clause. Source: © UNCTAD, IIA Mapping Project. Based on 2'538 mapped BITs signed between 1959 and 2016 (Id)

2.3.2 What Does the 'in Accordance with Host States' Laws' Clause Mean?: A Jurisprudential Analysis

Despite increasing attention to the 'legality' clauses in IIAs, there is still great uncertainty in the scope of their application. Certain tribunals have previously suggested limitations on the range of domestic laws with which an investor is expected to comply. These limitations could hamper States' attempts to rely on investor illegality for dismissing an arbitral claim.[72]

Tribunals applying an IIA an '*in accordance with host State law*' clause, an investment that was in violation of host State law did not enjoy the protection of the BIT.[73] However, even where tribunals had to apply an IIA without such clause in their text, they would refuse to grant protection to investments not respecting host State law. For instance, the Tribunal in *Plama* was bound by the Energy Charter Treaty which does not contain an *'in accordance with host State law clause'*. It decided, however, that the existence of such a clause is not a prerequisite for a tribunal to be able to deny protection to an illegal investment.[74] The tribunal took note of this absence, but stated: *'This does not mean, however, that the protections provided for by the ECT cover all kinds of investments, including those contrary to domestic or international law.'*[75]

Similarly, the Tribunal in *Phoenix* adopted this approach by stating that '*this condition – the conformity of the establishment of the investment with the national laws – is implicit even when not expressly stated in the relevant BIT*'[76] The possibility to deny investment protection to illegal investments is limited, though, to illegalities committed by the investor. The host State can retain a degree of control over foreign investments, by accepting only those complying with its domestic laws.[77] As noted by the tribunal '*These treaties, however, do not allow a State to preclude an investor from seeking protection under the BIT on the ground that its own actions are illegal under its own laws. In other words, a host State cannot avoid jurisdiction under the BIT by invoking its own failure to comply with its domestic law.*'[78]

An ICSID tribunal may have to rule on the validity of a contract under the national laws of the host state or may have to consider which rights are granted, or not granted, to the investor under domestic law.[79] This section focuses on the

---

[72] Hepburn (2014).

[73] Kriebaum (2010), p. 2.

[74] *Plama Consortium Limited v. Bulgaria*, ICSID Case No. ARB/03/24, Award, 27 August 2008, paras. 219–221.

[75] Id., para 138.

[76] *Phoenix Action, Ltd. v. Czech Republic*, ICSID Case No. ARB/06/5, Award, 15 April 2009, para 101.

[77] Kriebaum (2010) id., p. 2.

[78] Ibid.

[79] Dolzer and Schreuer (2012), p. 64.

meaning of the legality requirement, reflected or not in the respective IIAs, examining the interpretations adopted by different tribunals.

2.3.2.1 Law of the Host State as a Whole

Certain cases have interpreted the legality requirement, by making reference to the law of the host State as a whole.[80] For instance, in the case of *Aguas del Tunan,* the tribunal dismissed Bolivia's argument and observed that the '*Respondent's interpretation would permit a host State to take its affirmative responsibility to 'promote economic cooperation through the protection of investments of nationals of the other Contracting Party in its territory' and to transform it into an opportunity to introduce exclusive local jurisdiction for investment disputes'*[81] The Bolivia-Netherlands BIT contained a reference to local law regarding the promotion and admission of investments. Examining these aspects separately, the tribunal concluded, in respect of the former, that reference to the State's '*framework of its laws and regulations'* was '*limited to the details of how each contracting party undertakes to promote economic cooperation in its national laws and regulations through the protection of investments'*[82]; and, in respect of the latter, that '*the reference specifically subjects the State's duty to admit investments not to the laws and regulations of Bolivia, but rather to the 'right to exercise powers' conferred by such laws and regulations'*.[83]

2.3.2.2 Fundamental Principles of Law

A different approach doesn't require investors to comply with all of the host State's law. In *LESI v Algeria,* the tribunal accepted that investments would lose treaty protection only when made *'in violation of fundamental principles in force.'*[84] A similar view was adopted by the tribunals, later on, in the cases *Desert Line v Yemen*[85] *and Rumeli v Kazakhstan.*[86] They both accepted that investor legality only related to breaches of *'fundamental principles of the host State's law.'*[87]

[80]Carlevaris (2008) id. pp. 35–49.

[81]*Aguas del Tunari S.A. v. Republic of Bolivia* (Aguas del Tunan), Decision on Respondent's Objections to Jurisdiction, 21 October 2005, para 153.

[82]Ibid., para 153.

[83]Id., para 147.

[84]*LESI SpA and Astaldi SpA v Algeria*, ICSID Case No ARB/05/3), Decision on Jurisdiction, 12 July 2006.

[85]*Desert Line Projects LLC v Yemen*, ICSID Case No ARB/05/17), Award, 6 February 2008.

[86]*Rumeli Telekom AS v Kazakhstan*, ICSID Case No ARB/05/16), Award, 29 July 2008.

[87]Hepburn (2014) id.

This approach, though, is highly doubted by scholars.[88] The wording of IIAs does not limit its scope to 'fundamental principles', rather mentioning generally 'host State's law'. Indeed, in *Quiborax v Bolivia,* the tribunal expressly rejected the claimant's support for a *'fundamental principles'* limitation, considering that it went *'beyond the terms of the BIT, in an attempt to further the investor's protection without due regard for the State's interests.'*[89] Tribunals, though, would not decline jurisdiction for a trivial breach of local law. For instance, in *Alpha Projektholding v Ukraine,* the minor defect in company paperwork at issue in was not sufficient to exclude the tribunal's jurisdiction.[90]

It remains, therefore, up to the interpretation by the competent tribunals to decide upon the nature of domestic laws and regulations the investor in each specific case has to comply with.

2.3.2.3 Laws Related to Investment

Another approach prioritizes laws of the host State directly related to the investment at stake. For instance, in *Saba Fakes v Turkey*, the tribunal commented that Turkey's claim of the investor's non-compliance with domestic competition law and telecommunications regulatory law was irrelevant, because these were not laws '*related to the very nature of investment regulation.*' Thus, the legality provision only required compliance with laws '*governing the admission of investments in the host State.*'[91]

However, no such specific reference is explicitly made in any IIA, and no other tribunal has considered the subject-matter of the law allegedly breached by an investor to be relevant. In *Anderson v Costa Rica*[92] and *Hamester v Ghana,*[93] the tribunal took into account the alleged breaches of domestic criminal law on fraud, even if they addressed a wide range of actors and situations. In *Vannessa Ventures v Venezuela,* where the claimant explicitly followed the approach of *Fakes* in its submissions, the tribunal avoided to analyse the question, finding simply that no Venezuelan laws had been breached.[94] Based on the above, the approach of restricting the legality requirement only to investment-related laws doesn't seems to be sufficiently justified.

[88] Ibid.

[89] *Quiborax SA v Bolivia*, ICSID Case No ARB/06/2, Decision on Jurisdiction, 27 September 2012.

[90] *Alpha Projektholding GmbH v Ukraine*, ICSID Case No ARB/07/16, Award, 8 November 2010.

[91] *Saba Fakes v Turkey*, ICSID Case No ARB/07/20, Award, 14 July 2010, paras. 119–120.

[92] *Alasdair Ross Anderson et al v. Republic of Costa Rica*, ICSID Case No. ARB(AF)/07/3.

[93] *Gustav F W Hamester GmbH & Co KG v. Republic of Ghana*, ICSID Case No. ARB/07/24.

[94] *Vannessa Ventures Ltd v Venezuela*, ICSID Case No ARB(AF)/04/6, Award, 16 January 2013, paras 132, 135, 154, 160, 164, 167.

2.3.2.4 The Good Faith Principle

A broader interpretation of the 'legality requirement' requires the investor to comply with fundamental, general principles of law in the abstract, such as good faith, international public policy and prohibitions of fraud, corruption and deceit.[95] A question in this respect is whether, a breach of the good faith principle can remove the case even if there is no obvious breach of the host State's law.

In the *Inceysa v. El Salvador* case, the tribunal, examining the aspects of the investment in its acquisition but also in its performance,[96] stated the following:

> [g]eneral principles of law are an autonomous and direct source of International Law, along with international conventions and custom. (...) Based on the above, we analyze the Inceysa's investment in light of the general principles of law, which the Arbitral Tribunal considers to be applicable to the case. (...) Good faith is a supreme principle, which governs legal relations in all of their aspects and content. (...) The conduct mentioned above constitutes an obvious violation of the principle of good faith that must prevail in any legal relationship. (...) By falsifying the facts the principle of good faith from the time it made its investment and, therefore, it did not make it in accordance with Salvadoran law. Faced with this situation, this tribunal can only declare its incompetence to hear Inceysa's complaint, since its investment cannot benefit from the protection of the BIT.[97]

Another example comes from the Israel–Uzbekistan BIT, which defines 'investment' as meaning '*any kind of assets, implemented in accordance with the laws and regulations*' of the host state.[98] In *Metal-Tech v. Uzbekistan* case, the tribunal interpreted the above-mentioned clause as referring to the laws and regulations existing at the time the investment was made.[99] This means that the investment should be in compliance with the law at the time when it was established. Otherwise, it would not be subject to the protection of the BIT and would, thus, be dismissed from the tribunal's jurisdiction.

As analysed by the tribunal, the fact that two of the consulting agreements were made through corruption affected the legality of the establishment of the investment, which was thus not '*implemented in accordance*' with the laws of Uzbekistan. It held that '*Uzbekistan's consent to ICSID arbitration, as expressed in Article 8(1) of the BIT, is restricted to disputes concerning an investment, as defined in Article 1(1) of the BIT*'.[100] As stated, the dispute did not '*come within the reach of Article 8(1) and [was] not covered by Uzbekistan's consent*'.[101] The tribunal, thus, declared that it lacked jurisdiction over the dispute. Therefore, according to the tribunal's

---

[95] Hepburn (2014).

[96] Dajić (2012), p. 220.

[97] *Inceysa Vallisoletana S.L. v. Republic of El Salvador*, ICSID Case No. ARB/03/26, Decision on Jurisdiction of 2 August 2006, paras. 226, 229, 230, 237, 239.

[98] Agreement between the Government of the State of Israel and the Government of the Republic of Uzbekistan for the promotion and reciprocal protection of investments, Article 1, para 1.

[99] *Metal-Tech Ltd. v. The Republic of Uzbekistan*, ICSID Case No ARB/10/3, para 193.

[100] Id., para 373.

[101] Ibid.

interpretation, illegality during the establishment of an investment must lead to a dismissal of jurisdiction. However, the tribunal remained silent on whether non-compliance with host State's laws after the establishment of the investment, that is, in the course of its operation, would lead to a similar or different consequence.[102]

As concerns corruption, the tribunal in *World Duty Free v. Kenya,* held that corruption is '*contrary to international public policy of most, if not all States, or to use another formula, to transnational public policy*'.[103] As concluded by Judge Lagergren:

> a case such as this, involving such gross violation of good morals and international public policy, can have no countenance in any court neither in the Argentine or in France, or, for that matter, in any other civilised country, nor in any arbitral tribunal. Thus, jurisdiction must be declined in this case.[104]

2.3.3 Conclusion

The application of the legality requirement, most commonly found in IIAs as '*in accordance with host State's law',* has been subject to different interpretations. Investment tribunals have distinguished between the law of the host State as a whole, fundamental principles of law, and laws related solely to the investment, while others have adopted a wider approach, including the good faith principle in their analysis. With an interpretation in accordance with the text, scope, and purpose of the respective IIA, the legality requirement can be added to the toolbox of States as a defensive mechanism against investment treaty claims, and, eventually, facilitate the enforcement of their sustainable development objectives.

References

Balisacan A, Chakravorty U, Ravago M-L (2014) Sustainable economic development: resources, environment, and institutions, 1st edn. AP Elsevier

Ballantyne J (2022) Poland moves to exit ECT. GAR. Available at: https://globalarbitrationreview.com/article/poland-moves-exit-ect

Barbier EB (1987) The concept of sustainable economic development. Environ Conserv 14(2): 101–110. https://doi.org/10.1017/S0376892900011449

Beirne J, Fernandez DG (2022) Harnessing digitalization for sustainable economic development: insights for Asia. Asian Development Bank Institute. Available at: https://www.adb.org/publications/harnessing-digitalization-sustainable-economic-development

[102] Id., para 193.

[103] *World Duty Free Company v Republic of Kenya*, ICSID Case No. Arb/00/7, para 157.

[104] Id., para 148.

Carlevaris A (2008) The conformity of investments with the law of the host state and the jurisdiction of international tribunals. J World Invest Trade 9(1). https://doi.org/10.1163/221190008X00304
Collins E, Sharpe J (2022) Obligations of the Host State. Jus Mundi. https://jusmundi.com/en/document/publication/en-obligations-of-the-host-state
Dajić S (2012) Mapping the good faith principle in international investment arbitration: assessment of its substantive and procedural value. Proceedings of the Faculty of Law in Novi Sad. 3/2012. https://doi.org/10.5937/zrpfns46-3011
Dang G, Pheng LS (2015) Infrastructure investment in developing economy. Springer Science Business Media Singapore. https://doi.org/10.1007/978-981-287-248-7_2
Dolzer R, Schreuer C (2012) Principles of international investment law, 2nd edn. OUP. https://doi.org/10.1093/law/9780199651795.001.0001
Garcia-Bolivar OE (2011) Economic development at the core of the international investment regime. In: Brown C, Miles K (eds) Evolution in investment treaty law and arbitration. CUP. https://doi.org/10.1017/CBO9781139043809
Gordon K, Pohl J (2011) Environmental concerns in international investment agreements: a survey. OECD Working Papers on International Investment, 2011/01, OECD Publishing. https://doi.org/10.1787/5kg9mq7scrjh-en
Grabowski A (2014) The definition of investment under the ICSID Convention: a defense of Salini. Chic J Int Law 15(1). Article 13
Hepburn J (2014) In accordance with which host state laws? Restoring the 'Defence' of Investor Illegality in Investment Arbitration. IISD. Available at: https://www.iisd.org/itn/en/2014/11/19/in-accordance-with-which-host-state-laws-restoring-the-defence-of-investor-illegality-in-investment-arbitration/
Kriebaum U (2010) Illegal investments. Austrian Yearbook on International Arbitration
Levashova L (2011) Role of sustainable development in Bilateral Investment Treaties: recent trends and developments. J Sustain Finance Invest 1:3–4. https://doi.org/10.1080/20430795.2012.655890
Mitchell AD, Munro J (2018) No retreat: an emerging principle of non-regression from environmental protections in international investment law. Geo J Int Law 50
Mukherjee S, Chakrabarti NK (2021) Is "contribution to the host states development" an essential criterion to define investment under international investment law?: A search through the lens of arbitral awards. Liverpool Law Rev 42:429–463. https://doi.org/10.1007/s10991-021-09282-3
Schefer KN (2013) International investment law: text, cases and materials. Edward Elgar Publishing Limited
Stern B (2011) The contours of the notion of protected investment. ICSID Rev Foreign Invest Law J

Chapter 3
Assessing the Existence of a Violation of an Investment Treaty

> Cultivating a mentality shift toward long-term investing is critical. Investors, both public and private, must shift their focus away from short-term advantages and toward long-term benefits of sustainable infrastructure. *(UN China (10 July 2023) Remarks by Mr. Ban Ki-moon at the Parallel Forum on Capital Mobilization for Sustainable Infrastructure at the First High-Level Conference of the Forum on Global Action for Shared Development.)—Ban Ki-moon*

Abstract This Chapter deals with the interpretation of relevant International Investment Agreements' (IIAs) provisions related to the treatment and protection of foreign investments. Following the establishment of jurisdiction, Investment Tribunals proceed to assess the merits of the case, examining whether there has been a violation of the applicable Investment Treaty. Asserted violations are assessed by ISDS tribunals against a series of standards of protection for foreign investors contained therein. In essence, IIAs standards of protection provide for specific obligations upon host States vis-à-vis foreign investors, namely: to provide fair and equitable treatment (FET), to abstain from illegal expropriation, and to avoid discrimination. Moreover, IIAs often provide for s.c. "Umbrella Clauses", whereby the protections are extended to any other contractual arrangements stipulated between the host State and the investor. The present Chapter investigates the interpretation and application of the above-mentioned standards of protection, as enshrined in IIAs, exploring their implications for sustainable development.

3.1 Fair and Equitable Treatment

The basic premise of international investment law is that investments abroad need to be protected against unfair and discriminatory treatment. The scope of application of this premise has a direct impact on the content of the measures taken by States.

M.-E. Konstantinidi, *Closing the Gap: Enhancing the Implementation of Sustainable Development through International Investment Law*, SpringerBriefs in Law,
https://doi.org/10.1007/978-3-031-73873-9_3

The FET clause protects the investor by assuring that the host-state maintains a stable and predictable investor climate that is in line with the investor's reasonable-legitimate expectations. The clause originates from the minimum standard treatment of foreigners (MST) that can be found in customary international law.[1] This clause is one of the main topics of debate in the current environmental debate amongst scholars, mainly due to the broad range of different and wide interpretations by tribunals along with the fact that it is usually the most successful basis for claims when changes in the host-states' national environmental law occur.

The obligation to provide fair and equitable treatment can be found in most BITs and other investment treaties. Taking for example Article 1105(1) of the North American Free Trade Agreement of 1992 ("NAFTA"), which stipulates that '*[e]ach Party shall accord to investments of investors of another Party treatment in accordance with international law, including fair and equitable treatment and full protection and security.*'[2]

FET clauses used in BITs and other IIAs appeared in early international economic agreements such as the Havana Charter for an International Trade Organization (1948) and the Economic Agreement of Bogotá (1948), as well as in the United States Friendship, Commerce and Navigation (FCN) treaties.[3] The first use of the FET clause in the IIA context can be traced back to Article I of the Draft Convention on Investments Abroad proposed by Hermann Abs and Lord Shawcross in 1959:

> Each Party shall at all times ensure fair and equitable treatment to the property of the nationals of the other Parties. Such property shall be accorded the most constant protection and security within the territories of the other Parties and the management, use and enjoyment thereof shall not in any way be impaired by unreasonable or discriminatory measures[4]

In 2007, the Tribunal in *PSEG v. Turkey* properly characterized the nature and role of the FET rule as follows:

> The standard of fair and equitable treatment has acquired prominence in investment arbitration as a consequence of the fact that other standards traditionally provided by international law might not in the circumstances of each case be entirely appropriate. This is particularly the case when the facts of the dispute do not clearly support the claim for direct expropriation, but when there are notwithstanding events that need to be assessed under a different standard to provide redress in the event that the rights of the investor have been breached.
>
> Because the role of fair and equitable treatment changes from case to case, it is sometimes not as precise as would be desirable. Yet, it clearly does allow for justice to be done in the absence of the more traditional breaches of international law standards. This role has resulted in the concept of fair and equitable treatment acquiring a standing on its own, separate and

---

[1] Brown and Miles (2011), p. 89; Article 1105 NAFTA & Article 10(1) ECT.

[2] North American Free Trade Agreement of 1992, 32 ILM 289, 605, [hereinafter NAFTA], art. 1105(1).

[3] UNCTAD (2011) *Scope and Definition*, UNCTAD Series on Issues in International Investment Agreements II, UN NY & Geneva.

[4] Abs and Shawcross (1960), pp. 115–124.

distinct from that of other standards, albeit many times closely related to them, and thus ensuring that the protection granted to the investment is fully safeguarded.[5]

3.1.1 Methodology of Applying the FET Rule

The literature conceptualising the FET standard on the basis of jurisprudence has proposed several criteria that impose conditions on the State's right to regulate.[6] For instance, certain sub-groups imposing conditions on the States' regulatory conduct include the following:

> (1) good faith in the conduct of a party; (2) consistency of conduct; (3) transparency of rules; (4) recognition of the scope and purpose of laws; (5) due process; (6) prohibition of harassment; (7) a reasonable degree of stability and predictability of a legal system; and, in particular (8) recognition of the legitimate expectations on the part of the investor.[7]

As regards the methodology of applying the standard of Fair and Equitable Treatment, more and more tribunals seem to prefer deploying a 'list approach' in their efforts to articulate their reasoning with more specificity, which seems to be an evolution of the above-mentioned criteria.[8] This means setting forth a list of components which, in their entirety, may compose the full reach of the FET standard.

The "list approach" was employed for the first time in *Tecmed v. Mexico (Tecmed)* as follows:

> The Arbitral Tribunal considers that this provision of the Agreement, in light of the good faith principle established by international law, requires the Contracting Parties to provide to international investments treatment that does not affect the basic expectations that were taken into account by the foreign investor to make the investment. The foreign investor expects the host State to act in a consistent manner, free from ambiguity and totally transparently in its relations with the foreign investor, so that it may know beforehand any and all rules and regulations that will govern its investments, as well as the goals of the relevant policies and administrative practices or directives, to be able to plan its investment and comply with such regulations [. . .] The foreign investor also expects the host State to act consistently, i.e. without arbitrarily revoking any preexisting decisions or permits issued by the State that were relied upon by the investor to assume its commitments as well as to plan and launch its commercial and business activities. The investor also expects the State to use the legal instruments that govern the actions of the investor or the investment in conformity with the function usually assigned to such instruments, and not to deprive the investor of its investment without the required compensation.[9]

---

[5] *PSEG Global, Inc., The North American Coal Corporation, and Konya Ingin Electrik Üretim ve Ticaret Limited Sirketi v. Republic of Turkey*, ICSID Case No. ARB/02/5.

[6] Levashova (2011), p. 9.

[7] Dolzer (2014), p. 15.

[8] *Ibid.*, pp. 13–14.

[9] *Tecnicas Medioambientales Tecmed S.A. v. United Mexican States*, ICSID Case No. ARB(AF)/00/2, Award, para 154 (May 29, 2003) [hereinafter Tecmed Award], 10 ICSID Rep. 134.

The *Tecmed* Award has been the award the most often cited in arbitral jurisprudence. However, other approaches may prefer an interpretation according to the VCLT standards. For instance, in *Rompetrol Group NV v. Romania*, the tribunal seems to agree with the 'list approach' but then proceed to state that it will '*follow the ordinary meaning of the words used, in their context, and in the light of the object and purpose of the BIT.*'[10]

3.1.2 Legitimate Expectations

One of the main elements of the fair and equitable treatment (FET) standard is the notion of legitimate expectations.[11] Actually, in 2012, the Tribunal in *Electrabel v. Hungary*[12] highlighted that '*the most important function*' of the FET standard is the protection of the investor's legitimate expectations[13]. To better define the notion, the research attempts to look deeper in the roots of 'legitimate expectations' and examines the different interpretations adopted by investment tribunals.

Taking a look at the definition of expectation in the Oxford English Dictionary, namely '*the action or fact of anticipating or foreseeing something; the belief that something will happen or be the case*',[14] it is obvious that it refers to something more than a mere hope in relation to the future.

Legitimate expectations are created by explicit undertakings on the part of the host State but also by undertakings of a more general nature.[15] These may include the legal framework of the host State, consisting of legislation and treaties, assurances contained in decrees, licenses, and similar executive statements, as well as contractual undertakings. Specific representations made explicitly or implicitly may also play an important role in the creation of legitimate expectations.[16] A reversal of such undertakings by the host State may result in the violation of an international investment treaty.

In *Thunderbird v Mexico*,[17] before reaching the conclusion that the investor's continued operation of gaming facilities in Mexico was not based on a legitimate expectation,[18] the Tribunal gave the following definition of legitimate expectations:

> Having considered recent investment case law and the good faith principle of international customary law, the concept of 'legitimate expectations' relates, within the context of the

[10] *The Rompetrol Group N.V. v. Romania*, ICSID Case No. ARB/06/3.

[11] Nahli et al. (2020), p. 26; Dolzer and Schreuer (2012), p. 115.

[12] *Electrabel S.A. v. Republic of Hungary*, ICSID Case No. ARB/07/19.

[13] Dolzer (2014) p. 17.

[14] Soanes (2010).

[15] Dolzer and Schreuer (2012), pp. 115, 145.

[16] *Ibid.*

[17] *Thunderbird v Mexico*, Award, 26 January 2006.

[18] *Id.*, para 208.

> NAFTA framework, to a situation where a Contracting Party's conduct creates reasonable and justifiable expectations on the part of an investor (or investment) to act in reliance on said conduct, such that a failure by the NAFTA Party to honour those expectations could cause the investor (or investment) to suffer damages.[19]

The threshold for legitimate expectations may vary depending on the nature of the violation alleged under the relevant investment agreement and the circumstances of the case. In a number of cases, due to their generality and the absence of specific reference in investment agreements, the mere existence of legitimate expectations on the part of investors is challenged.[20] However, arbitral tribunals are referring more and more often to the concept of legitimate expectations, taking them into consideration in the issuance of awards when reasonable and justifiable.[21] In the analysis below, the research focuses on the investors' general expectations for regulatory stability and consistency of the host State's legal order in an attempt to clarify when these expectations are considered legitimate.

3.1.3 Stability and Consistency of the Host State's Legal Order

Under the concept of legitimate expectations in international investment law, States are required to maintain a certain degree of stability and predictability in their regulatory framework, which is relied upon by investors when making investments.[22] Substantial changes to the host States' legal framework resulting in serious financial losses for the investors may give rise to claims of violation of the FET rule.

As concerns any sort of expectation for stability and predictability on the part of the investor, it is argued that an obligation for the host State to ensure such a regulatory framework only exists when explicitly mentioned in the relevant FET provision.[23] In the absence of such clear treaty language, it has been accepted by tribunals that international investment law does not provide a mechanism of stability insurance for investors[24] and, therefore, should not be equated to the 'freezing' of the regulatory framework of a host State. Besides, it is widely recognized that for the

---

[19] *Id.*, para 147.

[20] Dolzer (2014) p. 25; *Parkerings-Compagniet AS v. Republic of* Lithuania (ICSID Case No. ARB/05/8); *Gustav F W Hamester GmbH & Co KG v. Republic of Ghana* (ICSID Case No. ARB/07/24).

[21] Dolzer and Schreuer (2012), p. 151.

[22] Dolzer (2014), p. 20; Levashova (2020).

[23] Partial Dissenting Opinion of Professor Philippe Sands QC, ICSID Case No. ARB/16/41, 9 September 2021, para 21.

[24] *MTD Equity Sdn. Bhd and MTD Chile S.A. v Republic of Chile*, ICSID Case No. ARB/01/7, Decision on Annulment (21 March 2007), para 67; *Mobil Investments Canada Inc and Murphy Oil Corporation v Government of Canada (I)*, ICSID Case No. ARB(AF)/07/4, Decision on Liability and on Principles of Quantum (22 May 2012), para 153; *Hydro Energy 1 S.à r.l. and Hydroxana*

existence of such an obligation, a preambular aspiration cannot as such give rise to an actionable obligation.[25]

The need for consistency of the host State's conduct has also been accepted as basis for the creation of legitimate expectations.[26] As stated in *El Paso v Argentina*, the host State '*should not unreasonably modify the legal framework or modify it in contradiction with a specific commitment*'.[27] However, consistency may not be required under circumstances where the host State had convincing reason to change course. In the presence of serious exceptional reasons, as the climate emergency, the host State may reverse its previous decisions and pursue its interests under the new circumstances, requiring the investor to re-adapt its business activities.[28] Indeed, as concerns regulatory changes, the Tribunal's view in *Total v Argentina* stated that:

> changes to general legislation, in the absence of specific stabilization promises to the foreign investor, reflect a legitimate exercise of the host State's governmental powers that are not prevented by a BIT's fair and equitable treatment standard[29]

In an opposite direction, the Tribunal in *Occidental v Ecuador*[30] recognized an obligation not to alter the legal and business environment in which the investment has been made.[31] As noted by the tribunal, under the FET standard, '*there is an obligation not to alter the legal and business environment in which the investment has been made*'[32] and that the stability requirement is 'an objective requirement that does not depend on whether the Respondent has proceeded in good faith or not.'[33] However, as ruled by the majority of arbitral tribunals, the obligation for stability is not absolute and does not affect the States' right to exercise their sovereign power to legislate and to adapt their legal system to changing circumstances.[34] If the implemented measures do not surpass an acceptable margin of change, and do not fundamentally modify the legal framework for the investment, they are considered to be within the normal regulatory powers of the State.

Sweden AB v. Kingdom of Spain, ICSID Case No. ARB/15/42, Decision on Jurisdiction, Liability and Directions on Quantum (9 March 2020), para 584.

[25] Sands Dissent. (2021), para 20; *Cargill, Incorporated v. United Mexican States*, ICSID Case No. ARB(AF)/05/2, paras 289–290.

[26] *MTD v Chile S.A.*, para 163; *Jan Oostergetel and Theodora Laurentius v. The Slovak Republic*, UNCITRAL, 2006, para 224.

[27] *El Paso Energy International Company v. Argentine Republic* (ICSID Case No. ARB/03/15), para 364.

[28] Dolzer (2014), p. 21.

[29] *Total v Argentina*, Decision on Liability, 27 December 2010, para 164.

[30] *Occidental Petroleum Corporation and Occidental Exploration and Production Company v. Republic of Ecuador* (II) (ICSID Case No. ARB/06/11).

[31] *Id.*, para 191; Ortino (2018).

[32] *Occidental Exploration and Production Company v. Republic of Ecuador* (I), LCIA Case no. UN3467, Award, 1 July 2004, para 191.

[33] *Id.* para 186.

[34] Dolzer and Schreuer (2012), p. 148.

Some tribunals have '*requir[ed] a weighing of the Claimant's legitimate and reasonable expectations on the one hand and the Respondent's legitimate regulatory interests on the other*'[35] Others, have maintained the strict standard of absolute stability over the objections of dissenters. As one dissenting arbitrator opined in the *Renergy v. Spain* case, '*[t]he expectation of a relatively (or absolutely) immutable rate of return identified by the Majority is not supported by the evidence or the case-law. It is an approach that is neither legitimate nor reasonable.*'[36]

Another concept often used in the tribunals' reasoning as concerns legitimate expectations is that of the '*prudent investor*'. The concept of prudence is used throughout the law as a description of a standard of conduct owed to others. In the law of torts, the '*ordinary reasonably prudent man*' is well known for the careful conduct of his own actions in avoiding personal injury to others, both with respect to his actions and with respect to the foreseeability of their consequences.[37]

In the context of international investment law, not every change in the host State's legal system affecting foreign property equals to a violation of legitimate expectations. No such violation will occur if the change remains within the boundaries of normal adjustments customary in the host state and accepted in other states. Such changes are considered predictable for a prudent investor. For example, the Tribunal in *Methanex v United States*[38] found that certain new environmental regulations in California should have been foreseeable for the Canadian investor.

As ruled in *Isolux v. Spain*, an investor's legitimate expectations can only be considered violated if the new regulatory changes were not foreseeable by 'a prudent investor'.[39] In this case, the tribunal established that the investor had made his investments in a photovoltaic (PV) plant in 2012, at the time when Spain had already introduced significant modifications to the regime that regulates renewable energy. The investor could have foreseen that additional state reforms were coming. The tribunal also noted that the investor possessed specific knowledge that the feed-in tariffs introduced by the Spanish authorities would not last for the entire lifetime of his investments.[40]

In *Plama v Bulgaria* the tribunal concluded that a prudent investor should have been aware of the debates at the parliament relating to the potential changes of the relevant environmental law.[41] In *Chemtura v Canada*[42] and, more recently,

[35] Aydos et al. (2022), p. 54.

[36] *RENERGY S.à r.l. v. Kingdom of Spain*, ICSID Case no. ARB/14/18, para 48.

[37] *Westbrook v. Watts*, 268 S.W.2d 694, 698 (Tex. Ct. App. 1954); on reasonable expectations see Burns et al. (1985), pp. 11, 40.

[38] *Methanex v United States*, UNCITRAL, Award, 3 August 2005.

[39] *Isolux Netherlands, BV v. Kingdom of Spain*, SCC Case V2013/153, Award (17 July 2016) para 781.

[40] *Isolux v. Spain*, *id.*, para 787; See also *BayWa r.e. Renewable Energy GmbH and BayWa r.e. Asset Holding GmbH v. Spain*, ICSID Case No. ARB/15/16, Award, para 463.

[41] *Plama Consortium Limited v. Bulgaria*, paras 220, 267.

[42] *Chemtura Corporation v Government of Canada*, UNCITRAL, Award, 2 August 2010, para 149.

Occidental v Ecuador[43] and *Charanne v Spain*,[44] the tribunals reasoned that the claimants, as sophisticated investors in their respective industries, could not reasonably expect that no regulatory measures would be taken by the respective host States during the period relevant for their investment.[45]

Following the same reasoning, it can be argued that, as concerns energy transition measures, it could be foreseen at the time many fossil fuel investments were made that sooner or later States would take action to reduce GHG emissions and limit global warming. Scientific discoveries about the impact of fossil fuels to the environment and intergovernmental discussions on the need to prevent climate change made it obvious for a 'prudent investor' to expect the regulatory framework of their host State to be altered. Indeed, in *WMH v. Canada case,* the government of Canada defended its phase-out in part by arguing that WMH could not have expected that the federal regulations regarding coal-powered energy would provide a '*predictable future*', as an informed investor would have known that the State was contemplating further emission regulations.[46]

In sum, an important source of expectations on the part of the investor is the legal framework of the host country at the time of the investment. To the extent that the state of the law was transparent and did not violate minimum standards as concerns stability and predictability, no violation of the fair and equitable standard of protection can be proven.

3.1.4 Due Diligence

The extent to which a host State can adapt its laws and policies in order to achieve its sustainable development goals, without violating the FET standard, is highly affected by the way tribunals balance States' obligation for stability with the investor's due diligence. The degree of investor diligence is an important factor in the assessment of the 'reasonableness' or 'legitimacy' of investors' expectations.[47]

In ISDS jurisprudence, the investor's due diligence in the context of FET surpasses the risk-based business due diligence performed by a foreign investor for its own benefit. As noted in several arbitral awards, the investor's responsibility to conduct an investigation into the host State's regulatory framework, affects the State's ability to regulate in the service of public interest.[48]

[43] *Occidental v Ecuador*, para 383.

[44] *Charanne BV and Construction Investments SARL v Kingdom of Spain*, ECT Arbitration 062/2012 (SCC Rules), Award, 21 January 2016, para 507.

[45] Vinuales (2017).

[46] *Westmoreland Mining Holdings LLC v. Government of Canada*, ICSID Case No. UNCT/20/3, Statement of Defence, 26 June 2020, p. 11.

[47] Vinuales (2017), p. 369; Levashova (2019), pp. 237–239.

[48] Levashova (2019).

In *EcoOro* the tribunal stated that

> there must be an obligation on an investor claiming that its reasonable investment-backed expectations has been breached, to have undertaken its own due diligence before relying on any encouragement or support given by the Government in making its investment'[49], concluding that 'given Eco Oro's apparent failure to undertake any due diligence before relying on such representations as were made to it by Colombia, the Tribunal does not find Eco Oro had any distinct reasonable investment backed expectations that exploitation would be permitted in the entirety of the concession area.[50]

Regulatory change should take place within certain reasonable bounds to be an acceptable exercise of the States regulatory powers. However, there is significant room for changes in the conditions of regulated markets that a foreign investor is expected to assess and anticipate, as part of its due diligence exercise. In the absence of the latter, the ability for an investor to invoke an impairment of its 'reasonable' or 'legitimate' expectations is very limited.

3.2 Expropriation

3.2.1 BITs Expropriation Clause

The implementation of policies for the promotion of sustainable development requires legislative measures, including taxation and/or restriction of certain commercial activities, which may deprive foreign investors of their investments. If this deprivation is substantial and permanent or prevents the enjoyment of the investments' economic benefits,[51] the investors may claim damages for illegal expropriation of their property. Indeed, investors in the fossil energy sector, notably oil and coal companies, have recently brought, or threatened to bring, investment arbitration claims against States which put an end to their activity for the purpose of reaching their climate change objectives. Some examples of such claims are provided by the cases of *WMH v. Canada*,[52] *Uniper v. Netherlands*[53] and *RWE v. Netherlands*.[54] Irrespective of the outcome of the arbitration proceedings, the risk of being ordered to pay very substantial damages may have a 'chilling effect' on States, meaning that

[49] *Eco Oro Minerals Corp. v. Republic of Colombia* (ICSID Case No. ARB/16/41), para 681.

[50] *Eco Oro v. Colombia*, para 694.

[51] Dolzer and Schreuer (2012), p. 111.

[52] *Uniper SE, Uniper Benelux Holding B.V. and Uniper Benelux N.V. v. Kingdom of the Netherlands*, ICSID Case No. ARB/21/22.

[53] *Westmoreland Mining Holdings LLC v. Government of Canada*, ICSID Case No. UNCT/20/3.

[54] *AG and RWE Eemshaven Holding II BV v. Kingdom of the Netherlands*, ICSID Case No. ARB/21/4; Putter (2021).

they may hesitate to implement the energy transition measures needed to fight climate change and its consequences.[55]

Despite the apparent proximity of the States' police powers to its police force, the two are not adjacent. Deriving from the Greek word *πολιτεία* [politeia],[56] which refers to the rights of citizens and the formation of government, '*police powers*' refer to the capacity of the States to regulate behavior and enforce order within their territory for the promotion and maintenance of health, safety, morals, and general welfare of the public.[57]

In this context, an important question on allocating compensation to foreign investors for indirect expropriation is whether the measures taken by the host State were of general regulatory nature. It is argued, in favor of States' sovereignty, that compensation is not due when a governmental measure is part of a State's power to regulate the general welfare, the so-called *'police powers'* of the State.[58] In such case, it is exceptionally permitted to the host State to regulate in derogation of the international commitments it has undertaken under an IIA without incurring a duty to compensate.[59] The present section elaborates upon the current contours of the doctrine of police powers, and the circumstances under which it can be used as a defense on the part of States, offering a tool for the enforcement of sustainable development goals.

3.2.2 The Police Powers Doctrine

As an accepted principle of international law, a BIT clause stating '*protection against expropriation without compensation'* means that an investor should feel safe that the host-state will not confiscate their foreign assets without compensating them for loss of the property of the investment. The exercise by a state of its regulatory powers does not qualify as expropriation if the regulations pursue a legitimate purpose, are proportionate to the aim pursued and are adopted in accordance with due process and public interest.[60] In such case, no compensation is required. Aiming to facilitate energy transition and human rights protection, it will be investigated, with reference to arbitral case law and a specific focus on the '*police powers doctrine*', whether and when compensation is due after an act of expropriation.[61]

---

[55] UNCTAD/ITE/IIA/2007/3 (2007) *Investor-State Dispute Settlement and impact on investment rulemaking*, United Nations, New York and Geneva; Brown and Miles (2011) pp. 134–135, 139–140; van der Merwe (2020).

[56] Westerlink (1981); Martin (1981).

[57] Britannica (2019).

[58] Dolzer and Schreuer (2012), p. 120; Pellet (2015).

[59] Pellet (2015).

[60] For example: Article 1110 NAFTA and Article 13 ECT.

[61] On compensation for expropriation see: Dolzer and Schreuer (2012), pp. 296–297; Brown and Miles (2011), pp. 409–416.

According to the OECD, '*it is an accepted principle of customary international law that where economic injury results from a bona fide non-discriminatory regulation within the police power of the State, compensation is not required.*"[62] This principle has been recognised by investment treaty decisions and is now enshrined in certain trade and investment treaties.

For instance, the 2012 U.S. Model BITs states in the section dealing with expropriation that: '*Except in rare circumstances, non-discriminatory regulatory actions by a Party that are designed and applied to protect legitimate public welfare objectives, such as public health, safety, and the environment, do not constitute indirect expropriations.*'[63]

Furthermore, pursuant to article 3 of the EU-Canada Comprehensive Economic and Trade Agreement:

> For greater certainty, except in the rare circumstance when the impact of a measure or series of measures is so severe in light of its purpose that it appears manifestly excessive, non-discriminatory measures of a Party that are designed and applied to protect legitimate public welfare objective, such as health, safety and the environment, do not constitute indirect expropriations.[64]

However, going back in time, the police powers doctrine was propounded much earlier than its recognition by investment treaties.

The 1961 Harvard Draft Convention on the International Responsibility of States for Injury to Aliens already provided in Article 10(5) as follows:

> An uncompensated taking of property of an alien or a deprivation of the use or enjoyment of property of an alien which results from . . . the action of the competent authorities of the State in the maintenance of public order, health, or morality . . . shall not be considered wrongful, provided
>
> (a) it is not a clear and discriminatory violation of the law of the State concerned;
> (b) it is not the result of a violation of any provision of Article 6 to 8 of this Convention [denial of justice];
> (c) it is not an unreasonable departure from the principles of justice recognized by the principal legal systems of the world; and
> (d) it is not an abuse of the powers specified in this paragraph for the purpose of depriving an alien of his property.[65]

The doctrine was further endorsed in the Third Restatement of the Foreign Relations Law of the United States of 1987 in the following terms:

---

[62] OECD, "*Indirect Expropriation" and the "Right to Regulate" in International Investment Law*, OECD Working papers on International Investment, 2004/4 (Sept. 2004), (RLA-238), p. 5, n. 10.

[63] 2012 Model Bilateral Investment Treaty between the government of the United States of America and the Government of [Country] concerning the encouragement and reciprocal protection of investment, p. 41, Annex B, Expropriation, para. 4 (b).

[64] Comprehensive Economic and Trade Agreement between the European Union and Canada ("CETA") Annex 8-A, Expropriation, Article 3.

[65] Draft Convention on the International Responsibility of States for Injuries to Aliens (1961) 55 Am. J. Int'l 548, p. 562.

> A State is not responsible for loss of property or for other economic disadvantage resulting from bona fide general taxation, regulation, forfeiture for crime, or other action of the kind that is commonly accepted as within the police powers of states, if it is not discriminatory.[66]

In 1989, in *Too v Greater Modesto Insurance Associates,* the Iran-US Claims Tribunal added the element of good faith in its ruling:

> A state is not responsible for loss of property or for other economic disadvantage resulting from bona fide general taxation or any other action that is commonly accepted as within the police power of States, provided it is not discriminatory and is not designed to cause the alien to abandon the property to the State or to sell it at a distress price.[67]

3.2.3 The Police Powers Doctrine in Arbitral Case Law

Despite its widespread recognition as a customary international law principle, the police powers doctrine was not immediately accepted in investment treaty decisions. A more consistent inclusion of the principle, differentiating the exercise of police powers from indirect expropriation, only emerged after 2000.[68] Some decisions have relied on the jurisprudence of the European Court of Human Rights, based on Article 1 of Protocol 1 of the Convention[69], in view of addressing regulatory measures for the protection of public health.

In 1903, the Claims Commission in the *Bischoff Case*, in dismissing a claim for damages, held that:

> [c]ertainly during an epidemic of an infectious disease there can be no liability for the reasonable exercise of police power.[70]

In 2005, in *Methanex v. United States* case, the tribunal held that:

> [A]s a matter of general international law, a non-discriminatory regulation for a public purpose, which is enacted in accordance with due process and, which affects, inter alios, a foreign investor or investment is not deemed expropriatory...[71]

In 2002, in *Tecmed v. Mexico* the tribunal stated:

> The principle that the State's exercise of its sovereign power within the framework of its police power may cause economic damage to those subject to its powers as administrator without entitling them to any compensation whatsoever is undisputable.[72]

---

[66] American Law Institute, Restatement (Third) Foreign Relations of the United States (1987), vol. 1, (RLA-257), para 712, comment (g).

[67] *Too v Greater Modesto Insurance Associates*, Iran-US CTR 23, p. 378, para 26.

[68] Bernasconi-Osterwalder et al. (2018), Bernasconi-Osterwalder and Johnson (2011).

[69] *Philip Morris Brands Sàrl, Philip Morris Products S.A. and Abal Hermanos S.A. v. Oriental Republic of Uruguay*, ICSID Case No. ARB/10/7, p. 83, para 295.

[70] Reports of International Arbitral Awards (1903) *Bischoff Case*, vol X, United Nations, p. 420.

[71] *Methanex Corporation v. United States of America*, UNCITRAL, Final Award of the Tribunal on Jurisdiction and Merits, Part IV, Chap. D, para 7.

[72] *Técnicas Medioambientales Tecmed, S.A. v. The United Mexican States*, ICSID Case No. ARB (AF)/00/2 Tecmed, para 122.

In *Chemtura v. Canada*, where a U.S. manufacturer of lindane, claimed a breach of the NAFTA by Canada's prohibition of its sale, the tribunal upheld the police powers doctrine, stating that:

> Irrespective of the existence of a contractual deprivation, the Tribunal considers in any event that the measures challenged by the Claimant constituted a valid exercise of the Respondent's police powers. As discussed in detail in connection with Article 1105 of NAFTA, the PMRA took measures within its mandate, in a non-discriminatory manner, motivated by the increasing awareness of the dangers presented by lindane for human health and the environment. A measure adopted under such circumstances is a valid exercise of the State's police powers and, as a result, does not constitute an expropriation.[73]

As concerns the scope, conditions and effects of the police powers doctrine the tribunal in *Saluka v. Czech Republic*, held the following:

> It is now established in international law that States are not liable to pay compensation to a foreign investor when, in the normal exercise of their regulatory powers, they adopt in a non-discriminatory manner bona fide regulations that are aimed to the general welfare'[74], adding that 'the principle that the State adopts general regulations that are 'commonly accepted as within the police power of States' forms part of customary international law today.[75]

A similar effect in the attribution of compensation was recognised in *EcoOro*:

> Given the measures were adopted as a part of Colombia's valid and legitimate exercise of its police powers [..] under international law, no compensation is payable.[76]

In the same award, it is worth noting the reference of the tribunal to Professor Sands' summary mentioning that

> any investor would have known that the general right of the State to act to protect the environment prevails over the narrower particular right of the investor where the State's resources are at issue and that a lawyer advising a reasonable investor would have had to say "I'm bound to alert you to the possibility that, because you are investing in an area that concerns nonrenewable resource, you are subject to an overriding interest of the State to protect other interests, including environmental interests.[77]

[73] *Chemtura Corporation v. Government of Canada*, UNCITRAL (formerly Crompton Corporation v. Government of Canada), Award, para 266.

[74] *Saluka Investments B.V. v. The Czech Republic*, UNCITRAL, Partial Award (Mar 2006), para 255.

[75] *Id.*, para 262.

[76] *Eco Oro Minerals Corp. v. Republic of Colombia*, ICSID Case No. ARB/16/41, para 698.

[77] *Eco Oro v. Colombia*, para 684.

3.2.4 The Case of Philip Morris v. Uruguay

Philip Morris v. Uruguay[78] and *Philip Morris v. Australia*[79] are among the prime examples of cases (together with *Vattenfall v. Germany (II)* case[80]) that provoked significant public awareness of the critical implications of investor–state dispute settlement and investment treaties.[81] In both cases, the investor challenged a good-faith regulation that seeks to mitigate undisputed public health risks linked to tobacco consumption.

To provide with a background, Uruguay has one of Latin America's highest smoking rates, with important implications for the Uruguayan economy and public health. In this context, in order to regulate tobacco consumption, Uruguay has engaged in important anti-smoking policy measures and adopted two principal regulations.

The first one, the Single Presentation Requirement regulation, which was adopted in 2008, provided that tobacco manufacturers could no longer sell multiple varieties of their brand. It also required health warnings to be printed on 50 per cent of the area of cigarette packages. Under a 2009 presidential decree, the second measure concerned the so-called "80/80 Regulation." According to this regulation, the health warnings were to cover 80 per cent, instead of 50 per cent, of the packaging, meaning that only 20 per cent could be used by the tobacco companies' trademarks and other information.[82]

These regulations had a great impact on the profits of Philip Morris, a company registered in Switzerland (under the names *Philip Morris Brands Sàrl* and *Philip Morris Products S.A.)* and investing in Uruguay through the Uruguayan company Abal Hermanos S.A. As a consequence, Philip Morris initiated arbitration proceedings against Uruguay for breach of its obligations under its bilateral investment treaty (BIT) with Switzerland, arguing that the measures taken by Uruguay constituted an indirect expropriation of its brand assets, including intellectual property and goodwill associated with each of its brand variants.[83] Uruguay's response was that the measures were a legitimate exercise of its sovereign police power to protect public health, and therefore, could not constitute an act of expropriation.[84]

The tribunal by unanimity agreed with Uruguay's argument acknowledging that the measure did not have the effect of substantial deprivation of the investment, since

---

78 *Philip Morris Brands Sàrl, Philip Morris Products S.A. and Abal Hermanos S.A. v. Oriental Republic of Uruguay*, ICSID Case No. ARB/10/7.

79 *Philip Morris Asia Limited v. The Commonwealth of Australia*, UNCITRAL, PCA Case No. 2012-12.

80 *Vattenfall AB and others v. Federal Republic of Germany(II)*, ICSID Case No. ARB/12/12; it should be noted that the parties eventually agreed to the discontinuance of the proceeding.

81 Bernasconi-Osterwalder et al. (2018), p. 43.

82 *Philip Morris v. Uruguay*, ICSID Case No. ARB/10/7.

83 *Id.*, para 180.

84 *Id.*, para181.

Philip Morris was able to continue its business of selling tobacco products in Uruguay. To further support its finding that there was no expropriation, the tribunal analysed the concept of police powers as reflected in previous jurisprudence.[85] As noted:

> the adoption of the Challenged Measures by Uruguay was a valid exercise of the State's police powers, with the consequence of defeating the claim for expropriation under Article 5(1) of the BIT.[86]

By reference to *Nicaragua v. United States* case, as concerns customary international law, the Tribunal stated that *'Article 5(1) of the BIT must be interpreted in accordance with Article 31(3)(c) of the VCLT requiring that treaty provisions be interpreted in the light of "[a]ny relevant rules of international law applicable to the relations between the parties," a reference "which includes ... customary international law."*[87]

Furthermore, '*[p]rotecting public health has since long been recognized as an essential manifestation of the State's police power, as indicated also by Article 2(1) of the BIT which permits contracting States to refuse to admit investments "for reasons of public security and order, public health and morality."*[88]

In other words, it was decided that despite the absence of any explicit reference to state police powers in the treaty, Article 5(1) of the BIT on expropriation should be interpreted in accordance with customary international law, including the police power doctrine. [89]

The tribunal concluded that Uruguay's measures, namely, the Single Presentation Requirement and the 80/80 Regulation, satisfied the conditions of the police power doctrine as they were adopted in good faith and for the purpose of protecting public health and were non-discriminatory and proportionate.[90] Following this reasoning, a State's reasonable bona fide exercise of police powers in matters of sustainable development, such as the maintenance of public order, health and morality, excludes compensation even when it causes economic damage to an investor and the measures taken for that purpose should not be considered as expropriatory.[91]

The decision in *Philip Morris v. Uruguay* has been extensively criticized on its analysis on the police powers doctrine.[92] Nevertheless, the importance accredited to international public health standards shows how investment tribunals can take a

---

[85] *Id.*, para 287.

[86] *Id.*, para 287.

[87] *Id.*, para 290.

[88] *Id.*, para 291.

[89] Mitchell (2018).

[90] *Philip Morris v. Uruguay*, p. 83, para 295.

[91] *Ibid.*

[92] Ranjan (2019), pp. 98–124; Radi (2018).

more systemic integration approach with the view of protecting and reinforcing the principles of sustainable development.[93]

In conclusion, expropriation claims arising out of measures relating to sustainable development policies may withstand arbitral scrutiny on the basis of the police powers doctrine, provided that they are adopted bona fide, in accordance with due process, as well as being non-discriminatory and proportionate. [94] Under these circumstances, the implementation of SDGs in national legislation is justified and, therefore, the States adopting the disputed measures do not have to pay compensation to the affected foreign investors.

3.3 Umbrella Clause

In order to hold a state responsible under international law, the prerequisite of violation of an international obligation can derive from the breach of the so-called 'umbrella clause' contained in the applicable bilateral or multilateral investment treaty.[95] The umbrella clause is a regular feature of investment treaties and calls for the observance of the obligations entered into by the host State. A typical version of a contemporary umbrella clause is article 10(1) ECT: '*Each Contracting Party shall observe any obligations it has entered into with an Investor or an Investment of an Investor of any other Contracting Party*'.[96]

The meaning of the umbrella clause concerning the type of obligations covered, as interpreted by different tribunals is quite vague and it is not entirely clear whether the meaning of these obligations implies the application of rules relevant to sustainable development principles, even if the latter have not been implemented to the host State's domestic laws.

3.3.1 Obligations Covered by an Umbrella Clause

It is estimated that approximately forty per cent of the existing investment treaties incorporate umbrella clauses.[97] These clauses typically bind the host State to uphold both investment treaty and non-investment treaty obligations. They may bring a wide range of obligations under the umbrella-like coverage of the investment treaty. Umbrella clauses may, for example, allow an extension of the treaty protection to obligations found in investment contracts, which specify the terms under which the

[93] Bernasconi-Osterwalder et al. (2018), p. 45.

[94] Vadi (2021); Pantelaki (2022).

[95] Dolzer and Schreuer (2012), p. 161.

[96] Energy Charter Treaty (1994) 2080 U.N.T.S., Art. 10.

[97] Yannaca-Small (2006), p. 5; Gill (2004), p. 397.

investment will take place. This would allow investors to enforce a wide variety of host State obligations— legislative, contractual, and treaty-based—through the investor–state dispute settlement mechanism.[98]

In *SGS v. Pakistan*, the tribunal rejected the argument that they had such broad powers, arguing that the legal consequences would be '*so far-reaching in scope, and so automatic and unqualified and sweeping in their operation, so burdensome in their potential impact upon a Contracting Party, we believe that clear and convincing evidence must be adduced by the Claimant . . .that such was indeed the shared intent of the Contracting Parties.*'[99]

However, subsequent tribunals have taken quite the opposite position. It is argued that the plain meaning of '*respecting any obligations made with respect to the investment'* is clear: it means all obligations, including contractual commitments and other obligations not based on the investment treaty itself.[100] This might mean that, for example, WTO law or the Aarhus Convention would become part of the obligations of an investment treaty.

In the case of *Allard v. Barbados,* the claimant, invoking Article 31(3)(c) of the VCLT, referred to Barbados' obligations under the United Nations Convention on Biological Diversity and the Ramsar Convention, in accordance with which Barbados designated the disputed swamp as a 'wetland of international importance.'[101]

In *Noble Ventures*, the tribunal held as to the meaning of the umbrella clause in the BIT between the United States and Romania that the wording and purpose of article of article II (2)(c) supported the interpretation that article II(2)(c) referred to investment contracts.[102] However, it was '*unnecessary for the Tribunal to express any definitive conclusion as to whether [. . .] Art. II(2)(c) of the BIT perfectly assimilates to a breach of the BIT any breach by the host State of any contractual obligation as determined by its municipal law or whether the expression 'any obligation', despite its apparent breadth, must be understood to be subject to some limitation in the light of the nature and objects of the BIT.*'[103]

In Eureko, it was argued that in light in light of the ordinary meaning, the context and the object and purpose of the umbrella clause in the BIT between the United States and Poland, article 3.5, every contractual obligation was protected; as stated:

> The plain meaning-the 'ordinary meaning'-of a provision prescribing that a State 'shall observe any obligations it may have entered into 'with regard to certain foreign investments is not obscure. The phrase, 'shall observe' is imperative and categorical. 'Any' obligations is capacious; it means not only obligations of a certain type, but 'any' - that is to say, all -

---

[98] *Ibid.*

[99] *SGS Société Générale de Surveillance S.A. v. Islamic Republic of Pakistan*, ICSID Case No. ARB/01/13.

[100] Bernasconi-Osterwalder et al. (2011); UNCTAD (2014) Investor-State Dispute Settlement. UNCTAD Series on Issues in International Investment Agreements II, UN NY & Geneva; *Siemens v. Argentina,* ICSID Case No. ARB/02/8, award, 6 February 2007, para 205.

[101] *Peter A. Allard v. The Government of Barbados*, PCA Case No. 2012-06.

[102] *Noble Ventures, Inc. v. Romania*, ICSID Case No. ARB/01/11, paras 51–52.

[103] *Id.*, para 61.

obligations entered into with regard to investments of investors of the other Contracting Party. [...] The context of Article 3.5 is a Treaty whose object and purpose is 'the encouragement and reciprocal protection of investment,' a treaty which contains specific provisions designed to accomplish that end, of which Article 3.5 is one.[104]

3.3.2 *Implications of Umbrella Clauses for Sustainable Development*

The concerns with umbrella clauses are straightforward: depending on their interpretation by tribunals, they may make desirable public welfare measures more costly and less likely to be enacted.[105] They may greatly expand the power of the protection that investment treaties offer to investors, at the same time shrinking the policy space governments may have to enact measures for purposes such as protection of the environment, health and safety.

Since the mechanism of ISDS only allows investor claims, leaving host States on the defendant's position, it is doubtful whether such claims can be used in favor of regulations enhancing sustainable development. A commonly accepted reality is that umbrella clauses may bring different commitments out of their originally intended legal frameworks to the ISDS mechanism. In addition, they may change the nature of State obligations under an investment treaty, making public welfare measures more likely to be found in breach of commitments on expropriation and FET.[106]

References

Abs H, Shawcross LH (1960) The proposed convention to protect private foreign investment. J Public Law 9

Aydos M et al (2022) Scaling investment in renewable energy generation to achieve sustainable development goals 7 (affordable and clean energy) and 13 (climate action) and the Paris Agreement: roadblocks and drivers. Columbia Center on Sustainable Investment

Bernasconi-Osterwalder N, Johnson L (ed) (2011) International investment law and sustainable development: key cases from 2000–2010. IISD. Available at: https://www.iisd.org/library/international-investment-law-and-sustainable-development-key-cases-2000-2010

Bernasconi-Osterwalder N et al (2011) Investment treaties and why they matter to sustainable development: questions and answers. IISD. Available at: https://www.iisd.org/publications/investment-treaties-and-why-they-matter-sustainable-development-questions-and-answers

Bernasconi-Osterwalder N, Dietrich Brauch M, Schacherer S (2018) International investment law and sustainable development: key cases from the 2010s. IISD

[104] *Eureko B.V. v. Republic of Poland*, partial award, 19 August 2005, para 246. The tribunal in Siemens v. Argentina took similar view. See *Siemens v. Argentina*, ICSID Case No. ARB/02/8, award, 6 February 2007, para 205.

[105] Bernasconi-Osterwalder et al. (2011), p. 34.

[106] Bernasconi-Osterwalder et al. (2011), p. 32.

Britannica T., Editors of Encyclopaedia (2019) 'police power'. Encyclopedia Britannica, Available at: https://www.britannica.com/topic/police-power

Brown C, Miles K (eds) (2011) Evolution in investment treaty law and arbitration. Cambridge University Press. https://doi.org/10.1017/CBO9781139043809

Burns RE et al (1985) The prudent investment test in the 1980s. The National Regulatory Research Institute. Available at: https://ipu.msu.edu/wp-content/uploads/2016/12/Burns-Prudent-Investment-Test-84-16-85-1.pdf

Dolzer R (2014) Fair and equitable treatment: today's contours. Santa Clara J Int Law 7/12. http://digitalcommons.law.scu.edu/scujil/vol12/iss1/2

Dolzer R, Schreuer C (2012) Principles of international investment law, 2nd edn. Oxford University Press. https://doi.org/10.1093/law/9780199651795.001.0001

Gill J (2004) Contractual claims and bilateral investment treaties. J Int Arbitr 21(5):397–412. https://doi.org/10.54648/joia2004025

Levashova Y (2011) Role of sustainable development in bilateral investment treaties: recent trends and developments. J Sustain Finance Investment 1:3–4. https://doi.org/10.1080/20430795.2012.655890

Levashova Y (2019) The right of states to regulate in their public interest and the right of investors to receive fair and equitable treatment. Kluwer Law International

Levashova Y (2020) The role of investor's due diligence in international investment law: legitimate expectations of investors. Kluwer Arbitration Blog. Available at: http://arbitrationblog.kluwerarbitration.com/2020/04/22/the-role-of-investors-due-diligence-in-international-investment-law-legitimate-expectations-of-investors/

Martin R (1981) The ideal State in Plato's 'Republic'. Hist Polit Thought 2(1):1–30. http://www.jstor.org/stable/26211766

Mitchell K (2018) Philip Morris v Uruguay: an affirmation of 'Police Powers' and 'Regulatory Power in the Public Interest' in International Investment Law. Ejil:Talk. Available at: https://www.ejiltalk.org/philip-morris-v-uruguay-an-affirmation-of-police-powers-and-regulatory-power-in-the-public-interest-in-international-investment-law/

Nahli R et al (2020) The debate surrounding the definition and legal basis of the legitimate expectations in investor-state dispute. Glob J Polit Sci Adm 8(1), ECRTD-UK

Ortino F (2018) The obligation of regulatory stability in the fair and equitable treatment standard: how far have we come? J Int Econ Law 21(4):845–865, 846–847, 851

Pantelaki M (2022) Defenses against investment treaty claims in pandemic times: fitting new trends into old standards. ITA Rev 4(2) https://itainreview.org/articles/2022/vol4/issue2/defenses-against-investment-treaty-claims-in-pandemic-times-fitting-new-trends-into-old-standards.html

Pellet A (2015) Police powers or the state's right to regulate. In: Kinner M (ed) Building International investment law: the first 50 years of ICSID. Kluwer Law International. Chap. 32

Putter S (2021) The Netherlands coal phase-out and the resulting (RWE and Uniper) ICSID arbitrations. Kluwer Arbitration Blog. Available at: http://arbitrationblog.kluwerarbitration.com/2021/08/24/the-netherlands-coal-phase-out-and-the-resulting-rwe-and-uniper-icsid-arbitrations/0

Radi Y (2018) Philip Morris v Uruguay: regulatory measures in international investment law: to be or not to be compensated? ICSID Rev Foreign Investment Law J 33(1):74–80. https://doi.org/10.1093/icsidreview/six031

Ranjan P (2019) Police powers, indirect expropriation in international investment law, and Article 31(3)(c) of the VCLT: A Critique of Philip Morris v. Uruguay. Asian J Int Law 9(1):98–124. https://doi.org/10.1017/S2044251318000139

Soanes C (2010) Oxford English Dictionary, 3rd edn. Oxford University Press

Vadi V (2021) Crisis, continuity, and change in international investment law and arbitration. Mich J Int Law 42:321–350

Merwe B van der (2020) Why investor lawsuits could slow the energy transition. EnergyMonitor Available at: https://www.energymonitor.ai/policy/international-treaties/why-investor-lawsuits-could-slow-the-energy-transition

Vinuales JE (2017) Investor diligence in investment arbitration: sources and arguments. ICSID Rev Foreign Investment Law J 32(2):346–370. https://doi.org/10.1093/icsidreview/siw041

Westerlink LG (1981) The title of Plato's Republic. Ill Class Stud 6(1):112–115. http://www.jstor.org/stable/23061976

Yannaca-Small K (2006) Interpretation of the Umbrella Clause in Investment Agreements. OECD Working Papers on International Investment, 2006/03. OECD Publishing. https://doi.org/10.1787/415453814578

Chapter 4
The Way Forward

> Our biggest challenge in this new century is to take an idea that seems abstract - sustainable development - and turn it into a daily reality for all the world's people. *(UN Information Service Vienna (14 March 2001). Secretary-General calls for break in political statement over environmental issues. SG/SM/7739-ENV/DEV/561)—Kofi Annan*

Abstract This Chapter draws on the previous Chapters to explore strategies and pathways to advance sustainable development through the intricate landscape of International Investment Law. First, it underscores the urgent need for reform in International Investment Agreements (IIAs) to better align with sustainable development objectives, emphasizing the importance of enhancing provisions that promote environmental protection, public health, and social welfare. Moving forward, it navigates the interpretation of IIAs within the context of sustainable development. It analyzes how arbitral tribunals approach and apply treaty provisions to balance investors' rights with States' regulatory prerogatives and public policy objectives. Lastly, it examines the background and qualifications of arbitrators assigned with resolving investment disputes, emphasizing the significance of diverse expertise and perspectives for ensuring fair and impartial decision-making. By addressing these key areas, this Chapter aims to offer insights and actionable recommendations for enhancing the role of International Investment Law in advancing sustainable development agendas, ultimately contributing to closing the gap between economic growth and environmental and social well-being.

4.1 Rethinking IIAs to Enhance Sustainable Development

With an increasing trend among States to draft more comprehensive agreements that rectify past misinterpretations and introduce innovations, their original intent is being reaffirmed. As for existing treaties, past errors can be rectified through an

M.-E. Konstantinidi, *Closing the Gap: Enhancing the Implementation of Sustainable Development through International Investment Law*, SpringerBriefs in Law,
https://doi.org/10.1007/978-3-031-73873-9_4

amendment procedure.[1] This requires that all treaty parties agree to renegotiate and subsequently reach a consensus on the amended text. Some treaties explicitly outline procedures for their amendment in their provisions.[2] Integrating provisions that reinforce States' rights to regulate within IIAs would strengthen the framework for implementing Sustainable Development Goals (SDGs).[3] Lower-income countries and civil society should also be taken into account in driving the reform agenda to ensure that their concerns and aspirations are adequately addressed.[4]

To enhance alignment with sustainable development objectives, IIAs could adopt a more holistic approach to investment governance, focusing on overcoming barriers to investment and promoting cross-border flows aligned with States' development priorities.[5] This approach involves not only addressing legal barriers but also identifying and mitigating practical challenges that hinder investment in sectors critical to sustainable development. Additionally, IIAs should discourage investments with detrimental impacts, such as those in fossil fuel extraction, corrupt dealings, or violations of labor standards.[6] By incorporating provisions that discourage such investments and incentivize those contributing positively to sustainable development, IIAs can play a more proactive role in advancing environmental protection, social welfare, and economic growth. Essential guiding principles for IIAs should include safeguarding policy space, preventing harm, advancing labor standards and environmental protection, fostering increased investment flows, and ensuring coherence across relevant policy spheres.[7] Additionally, IIAs should be flexible and adaptable to evolving challenges and circumstances, allowing for adjustments to be made to align with emerging priorities and global developments.

In instances where agreement for amendment cannot be reached, or where States determine that the disadvantages of remaining party to an IIA outweigh the benefits, withdrawal or termination of the treaty becomes an option.[8] If bilaterally agreed, this can be executed legally without breaching international law, following certain procedures often provided by the text of the treaty itself.[9] However, provisions of the agreement often remain in effect for a specified period for existing investments, commonly stipulated in 'sunset clauses'. Notably, several countries have initiated the termination of their Bilateral Investment Treaties (BITs) citing, amongst others, concerns over investor-state dispute settlement mechanisms and the preservation of

[1] Tienhaara and Cotula (2020); Bonafé and Piebalgs (2017).

[2] Bernasconi-Osterwalder et al. (2011) p. 47.

[3] UNCTAD (2011) Best practices in investment for development – how to prevent and manage investor-state disputes: lessons from Peru.

[4] Cotula (2014).

[5] Johnson et al. (2019); Porterfield et al. (2020).

[6] Johnson et al. (2019).

[7] Johnson (2015).

[8] Vienna Convention on the Law of the Treaties (1969) Art. 54.

[9] Bernasconi-Osterwalder et al. (2020); Juillard (2001), p. 2.

policy space for sustainable development initiatives.[10] Similarly, certain European Union (EU) countries have opted to withdraw from the Energy Charter Treaty (ECT) due to perceived inconsistencies with environmental and climate objectives.[11]

As the global community increasingly recognizes the imperative to align investment practices with sustainable development imperatives, rethinking IIAs to prioritize environmental protection, social welfare, and public policy space remains an ongoing endeavor. Collaboration among States, investors, and civil society is crucial to shaping IIAs that promote sustainable development goals while safeguarding the sovereignty of nations and the well-being of their citizens.

4.2 Interpretation of IIAs

Research suggests that investment treaty practice needs to change course. While the process of amending treaties can prove to be quite challenging, the interpretation of existing treaties offers a more flexible and efficient avenue for adapting to evolving circumstances.[12] Instead of reading new treaties like old ones, there is a growing recognition that the interpretation of older treaties should be guided by the object and purpose of more recent agreements. This approach allows for the resolution of legislative gaps and the generation of new outcomes that better reflect contemporary priorities and understandings.[13]

States have various mechanisms at their disposal to clarify terms in IIAs and ensure consistent interpretation. One such mechanism involves the issuance of joint or unilateral interpretative statements.[14] According to the Vienna Convention on the Law of Treaties (VCLT), interpretative statements can be made both before and after the treaty enters into force, as outlined in Articles 31(2) and 31(3) of the VCLT.[15] For example, in the context of NAFTA, interpretative statements were issued by the parties regarding the scope of the Fair and Equitable Treatment (FET) clause. These

[10] Hartmann and Spruk (2023); Bernhard (2023) Gathii (2019); Bhuta (2021); Olivet (2017).

[11] ECT News (2023) Written notifications of withdrawal from the Energy Charter Treaty. https://www.energycharter.org/media/news/article/written-notifications-of-withdrawal-from-the-energy-charter-treaty/. ECT News (2023) Written notification of withdrawal from the Energy Charter Treaty. https://www.energycharter.org/media/news/article/written-notification-of-withdrawal-from-the-energy-charter-treaty/. EC News (2023) European Commission proposes a coordinated EU withdrawal from the Energy Charter Treaty. https://energy.ec.europa.eu/news/european-commission-proposes-coordinated-eu-withdrawal-energy-charter-treaty-2023-07-07_en.

[12] Weeramantry (2012); Kammerhofer (2021); Fitzmaurice (2010).

[13] Alschner and Sarminento (2022). However, 'if investors can convince tribunals that older and more open treaty formulations are more protective towards investors, arbitrators would continue to interpret the standard in a more open way, despite treaty reforms'. See Alschner (2022), p. 129.

[14] Dolzer and Schreuer (2012), pp. 31–33.

[15] Bernasconi-Osterwalder et al. (2011), p. 48; Vienna Convention on the Law of the Treaties (1969) Art. 31(2), 31(3).

statements were subsequently accepted and applied by NAFTA tribunals, illustrating the impact of interpretative statements on treaty interpretation and application.[16]

Unilateral interpretative statements also play a role in clarifying treaty provisions. The International Law Commission has recognized the possibility for one or more parties to a treaty to issue a unilateral statement regarding the interpretation of its provisions. However, such statements must not be opposed by other parties to the treaty and must be consistent with the treaty's object and purpose. This mechanism provides States with a tool to offer their own interpretations of treaty provisions, contributing to a more transparent and predictable investment environment.[17]

4.3 Arbitrators' Background

Arbitrators in investment law disputes are responsible for interpreting and applying both the provisions of investment agreements and general international law, effectively performing a transnational law-making function.[18] Nonetheless, the limited of familiarity with human rights and environmental law among certain arbitrators in investor-state disputes has raised concerns for States and civil society. Ongoing studies are examining the impact of arbitrators' qualifications and background on investment awards, highlighting the need for greater expertise in areas such as human rights and environmental law within arbitral tribunals.[19]

One proposed solution involves the appointment of an independent expert to the arbitral tribunal, which would assist them with any human rights and related expertise.[20] This approach aims to enhance the tribunal's understanding of complex legal issues and ensure that decisions are informed by a broader spectrum of expertise. An interesting example of legislative action addressing this issue is the Dutch Model BIT of 2019. In Article 20(5), it states that the appointing authority shall make every effort to ensure that members of the tribunal either individually or together, '*possess the necessary expertise in public international law and that includes, amongst others, expertise in environmental and human rights law..*'.[21] This provision reflects a growing recognition of the importance of incorporating

---

[16] *Glamis Gold v. United States*, UNCITRAL, Award, June 8, 2009, para 599.

[17] Guiding Principles applicable to unilateral declarations of States capable of creating legal obligations, Text adopted by the International Law Commission (ILC) at its Fifty-eighth session, in 2006, and submitted to the General Assembly as a part of the Commission's report covering the work of that session (A/61/10). In: Yearbook of the International Law Commission (2006) vol. II, Part Two; See also NAFTA, Art. 1128.

[18] Titi (2013).

[19] Human Rights Council, Expert Mechanism on the Right to Development, Fifth session, *Right to development in international investment law,* Overview of the ongoing study by the Expert Mechanism on the Right to Development, A/HRC/EMRTD/5/CRP.2, pp. 9, 13.

[20] *Ibid.*

[21] 2019 Netherlands Model Bilateral Investment Treaty, Article 20 (5).

expertise in human rights and environmental law into investment dispute resolution processes.

It is interesting to note that Article 8.27(4) of the Comprehensive Economic and Trade Agreement (CETA) had already included a provision requiring expertise in public international law.[22] However, the Dutch Model BIT goes a step further by explicitly requiring experience that includes environmental and human rights law. While some may view this as controversial, particularly given the exclusion of provisions on sustainable development and corporate social responsibility from the investor-state dispute settlement (ISDS) provisions of the Model Treaty, it underscores the importance of ensuring that arbitral tribunals take into account disputes that might involve issues relating to sustainable development.[23]

In conclusion, efforts to enhance the expertise of arbitrators in human rights and environmental law represent a positive step towards ensuring fair and informed decision-making in investor-state dispute resolution processes. By incorporating diverse perspectives and expertise, arbitral tribunals can better address the multifaceted challenges posed by investment disputes and contribute to the promotion of sustainable development goals.

4.4 Concluding Remarks

Nowadays, the need to fight climate change and safeguard the rights of those in need has become a necessity. Yet, the international endeavour to render the UN Sustainable Development Goals a reality unfolds under limited resources. At the same time, the failure to hold accountable those responsible for environmental degradation and substandard living conditions shifts the cost of mitigation measures onto citizens.[24] Therefore, it is imperative that every available legal avenue be harnessed to pave the way for a more sustainable future.

Foreign investments play a pivotal role in advancing sustainable development. International investment arbitration, one of the most widely relied upon forms of alternative dispute resolution, as it offers a neutral and impartial forum for resolving disputes between foreign investors and host States. However, despite its benefits, investment arbitration faces mounting criticism due to issues such as inconsistency in arbitral awards and a lack of transparency. For the international investment arbitration system is to remain effective, it needs to be aligned with the Sustainable Development Goals.

Moreover, energy transition can be facilitated if States do not fear that their mitigation measures will backfire through investor-State disputes. The existence of

[22] Comprehensive Economic and Trade Agreement (CETA) between Canada, of the one part, and the European Union and its Member States, of the other part, Article 8.27 para 4.

[23] Human Rights Coucil, *id.*, p. 9.

[24] Berkes (1993), pp. 1–10.

strong defense mechanisms for States to counter fossil fuel investors' claims, and the appointment of Arbitrators with relevant background can foster the implementation of SDGs in domestic legislation. Additionally, political will to reform the existing system and the amendment of existing IIAs to cover 'sustainable' investments, would strengthen the respect of environmental and human rights obligations, and could incentivize renewable investors.

Several countries have already initiated policy reforms to address these challenges, and numerous tribunals have recognized the importance of sustainable development. However, whether existing mechanisms can effectively address sustainability concerns depends not only on the specific challenge at hand, but also on the dedication and creativity of adjudicators, as well as the receptiveness of judges to new, more human-centered approaches. Given that environmental protection is ultimately a matter of life and death, history will tell whether political leaders and societies can respond effectively to the efforts necessary to make the enforcement of the sustainable development goals a reality.

References

Alschner W (2022) Reversing innovation through MFN. In: Investment arbitration and state-driven reform: new treaties, old outcomes. OUP

Alschner W, Sarminento F (2022) An interview with Wolfgang Alschner on Investment Arbitration and State-Driven Reform: New Treaties, Old Outcomes. IISD. Available at: https://www.iisd.org/itn/en/2022/07/04/an-interview-with-wolfgang-alschner-on-investment-arbitration-and-state-driven-reform-new-treaties-old-outcomes-wolfgang-alschner-florencia-sarmiento/

Berkes F (1993) Traditional ecological knowledge in perspective. In: Traditional ecological knowledge: concepts and cases. J.T. Inglis. International Program on Traditional Ecological Knowledge, International Development Research Centre

Bernasconi-Osterwalder N et al (2011) Investment treaties and why they matter to sustainable development: questions and answers. IISD. Available at: https://www.iisd.org/publications/investment-treaties-and-why-they-matter-sustainable-development-questions-and-answers

Bernasconi-Osterwalder N et al (2020) IISD best practices series: terminating a bilateral investment treaty. International Institute for Sustainable Development

Bernhard W (2023) Denunciation of Bilateral Investment Treaties. JusMundi. Available at: https://jusmundi.com/en/document/publication/en-denunciation-of-bilateral-investment-treaties

Bhuta Z (2021) Pakistan to terminate 23 bilateral investment treaties. TheExpressTribune. Available at: https://tribune.com.pk/story/2313937/pakistan-to-terminate-23-bilateral-investment-treaties

Bonafé E, Piebalgs A (2017) The new international energy charter: sustainable energy transition, investment dispute resolution and market regulation. Florence School of Regulation European University Institute 33

Cotula L (2014) Investment treaties and sustainable development: investor-state arbitration. IIED. Available at: https://www.iied.org/17241iied

Dolzer R, Schreuer C (2012) Principles of international investment law, 2nd edn. Oxford University Press. https://doi.org/10.1093/law/9780199651795.001.0001

Fitzmaurice M (2010) On the interpretation of treaties: the modern international law as expressed in the 1969 Vienna Convention on the law of treaties. Am J Int Law 104(2):329–334

Gathii J T (2019) Understanding Tanzania's termination of Its BIT with the Netherlands in context. Afronomics Law. Available at: https://www.afronomicslaw.org/2019/04/01/understanding-tanzanias-termination-of-its-bit-with-the-netherlands-in-context
Hartmann S, Spruk R (2023) The impact of unilateral BIT terminations on FDI: quasi-experimental evidence from India. Rev Int Organ 18:259–296. https://doi.org/10.1007/s11558-022-09471-3
Johnson L (2015) Aligning Swiss investment treaties with sustainable development: an assessment of current policy coherence and options for future action. CCSI
Johnson L et al (2019) Aligning international investment agreements with the sustainable development goals. Columbia J Transnatl Law 58. https://doi.org/10.2139/ssrn.3452070
Juillard P (2001) Bilateral investment treaties in the context of investment law. OECD
Kammerhofer J (2021) Treaty interpretation. In: International investment law and legal theory: expropriation and the fragmentation of sources. CUP, pp 68–143
Olivet C (2017) Why did Ecuador terminate all its Bilateral investment treaties? TNI. Available at: https://www.tni.org/en/article/why-did-ecuador-terminate-all-its-bilateral-investment-treaties
Porterfield C et al (2020) Reforming the international investment regime through a framework convention on investment and sustainable development. CCSI
Tienhaara K, Cotula L (2020) Raising the cost of climate action? Investor-state dispute settlement and compensation for stranded fossil fuel assets. IIED. Available at: https://www.iied.org/17660iied
Titi C (2013) The arbitrator as a lawmaker: jurisgenerative processes in investment arbitration. J World Investment Trade 14(5):829–851. https://doi.org/10.2139/ssrn.2758113
Weeramantry JR (2012) Treaty interpretation in investment arbitration. OUP

The manufacturer's authorised representative in the EU is Springer Nature Customer Service Centre GmbH, Europaplatz 3, 69115 Heidelberg, Germany. If you have any concerns regarding our products, please contact ProductSafety@springernature.com

Printed and bound by CPI Group (UK) Ltd, Croydon, CR0 4YY
01/10/2026
02225880-0002